Philip H. Gordon

The Transatlantic Allies and the Changing Middle East

Routledge
Taylor & Francis Group

LONDON AND NEW YORK

Adelphi Paper 322

First published September 1998 by Oxford University Press for
The International Institute for Strategic Studies
23 Tavistock Street, London WC2E 7NQ

This reprint published by Routledge
2 Park Square, Milton Park, Abingdon, Oxon, 0 X 14 4RN
For the International Institute for Strategic Studies
Arundel House, 13-15 Arundel Street, Temple Place, London, WC2R 3DX
www.iiss.org

Simultaneously published in the USA and Canada
By Routledge
711 Third Avenue, New York, N Y 10017

Routledge is an imprint of the Taylor & Francis Group, an informa business

© The International Institute for Strategic Studies 1998

Director John Chipman
Assistant Editor Matthew Foley
Design and Production Mark Taylor

British Library Cataloguing in Publication Data
Data available

Library of Congress Cataloguing in Publication Data

ISBN 978-0-199-22377-0

contents

AIPAC	America–Israel Public Affairs Committee
Aramco	Arabian–America Oil Company
CFR	Council on Foreign Relations (US)
CFSP	Common Foreign and Security Policy
CIA	Central Intelligence Agency (US)
EC	European Community
EU	European Union
G-8	Group of Eight industrial nations
IGC	Intergovernmental Conference
ILSA	Iran and Libya Sanctions Act
IMF	International Monetary Fund
MENA	Middle East–North Africa economic-cooperation summit
NAC	North Atlantic Council
NATO	North Atlantic Treaty Organisation
NTA	New Transatlantic Agenda
OIC	Organisation of the Islamic Conference
OPEC	Organisation of Petroleum Exporting Countries
PA	Palestinian Authority
PLO	Palestine Liberation Organisation
UAE	United Arab Emirates
UNSCOM	UN Special Commission on Iraq
WMD	weapons of mass destruction
WTO	World Trade Organisation

introduction

Since the mid-1990s, US and European attitudes, strategies and policies towards the Middle East have diverged to a degree that frustrates the search for peace and damages transatlantic relations. Since the Oslo peace process began to break down in 1995, Europeans have grown frustrated with the near-monopoly on regional diplomatic action enjoyed by the US in the Arab–Israeli dispute, and have criticised perceived US partiality towards Israel. The appointment of a European Union (EU) coordinator for the Middle East peace process in October 1996, prominent visits to the region by European leaders and open European disagreement with the Israeli government's policies under Prime Minister Binyamin Netanyahu have demonstrated Europe's renewed desire to play a political role in the region. These developments have also led to tension and disagreement with the US over the future of the peace process, and over the measures required to move it forward.

Transatlantic tensions have been greater still in the Persian Gulf. The EU has opposed the US policy of Dual Containment, meant to deter and contain both Iraq and Iran. Europeans have generally been more willing to believe that Iran is changing for the better, and have maintained dialogue and trade with Tehran. They have also been more reluctant than the US to exert political and military pressure on Saddam Hussein's regime in Iraq, less willing to use or threaten military force in response to violations of UN resolutions, and opposed in principle to US attempts to force its strategic outlook for the region on a reluctant Atlantic Alliance.

When the US imposed a total economic boycott of Iranian goods in May 1995, and Congress in August 1996 passed legislation designed to punish foreign companies investing in Iranian and Libyan oil development, transatlantic relations over the Gulf deteriorated to possibly their lowest point in more than two decades.

Tension between the US and Europe in the Middle East is not, of course, a new phenomenon. US and European interests and strategies have clashed there since the 1950s, when the US began to displace the UK and France as the main outside power in the region. Differing views of Israel's security needs, the Soviet role in the Middle East and relations with oil-producing Muslim states formed the backdrop to sharp transatlantic disagreements over the Suez crisis of 1956, the Arab–Israeli wars of 1967 and 1973, Israel's 1982 invasion of Lebanon and the US bombing of Libya in April 1986. Current differences among the Atlantic allies on how to deal with the Arab–Israeli conflict and the Persian Gulf could therefore be seen as simply another episode in a series of NATO 'out-of-area' disputes. If Americans and Europeans disagree today on how to deal with Iran and Iraq, on whether to pressure Israel or on whether to recognise an independent Palestinian state, no one should be surprised.

If not new, however, transatlantic differences over the Middle East are detrimental to common Western interests – possibly even dangerous – for at least three reasons. First, divisions among the allies reduce the likely effectiveness of each side's policies. Washington's use of sanctions to *transatlantic differences* deny Iran resources, for example, *harm common interests* will have only a limited effect as long as Europe tries simultaneously to influence Tehran with trade, openness and a 'critical dialogue'. Economic sanctions – at best uncertain tools of statecraft – are more likely to succeed if implemented by a broad international coalition than if imposed by a single country, even one as strong as the US. On Iraq, the reluctance of certain European states, notably UN Security Council Permanent Members France and Russia, to support the use of force or other punitive measures makes it impossible for the US to create a united international front against the regime. Saddam's conviction that he could split the international coalition ranged against him probably led him to precipitate a crisis in late 1997–early

Map I *Israel and the Persian Gulf*

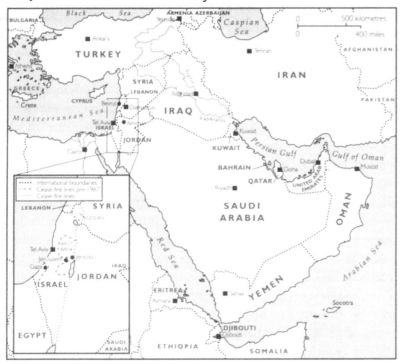

1998 by refusing to cooperate with weapons inspectors of the UN Special Commission (UNSCOM).

Many analysts argue that a harder line from one side of the Atlantic than the other can be useful in resolving crises. Some, for example, believed that French and Russian offers of compromise, together with the US-led threat to use military force, helped to defuse the arms-inspection crisis in February 1998. In fact, however, transatlantic differences usually hinder, rather than promote, the successful use of deterrence and diplomacy. A so-called 'good-cop/bad-cop' approach – when one set of allies takes a hard line, while another seeks engagement – may at times be unavoidable given the politics and preferences on each side of the Atlantic. This will, however, always be a second-best alternative to a united US–European front offering a combination of encouragement and restraint.

Transatlantic differences are also damaging because they undermine the cohesion of the Atlantic Alliance at a time when its unity is no longer guaranteed by a common threat. During the Cold War, quarrels over out-of-area issues did not significantly threaten NATO because the shared need to stand together always outweighed any extra-European disputes. With NATO's original *raison d'être* gone and the organisation occupied with optional issues rather than direct threats, differences between its members are more significant than in the past. It could be argued that NATO itself matters less than it did during the Cold War, but the Alliance's erosion during the first years of the Yugoslav civil war – and its rejuvenation once a common strategy was agreed – underlined both its vulnerability and its enduring value. It is right, therefore, to be concerned about NATO's future. If Americans come to see Europeans as free-riding appeasers of states that threaten global US interests, and Europeans see Americans as simplistic crusaders trying to assert unilateral authority over their allies, NATO's unity will be threatened. Many US analysts and officials see the organisation as a potentially anachronistic body unless it begins to address security problems beyond Europe's borders.[1] Should the Alliance succeed in pursuing common political, economic and military strategies, it will be a strong, credible and respected force in international politics. If it fails to do so it will wither.

Finally, transatlantic differences over the Middle East, particularly the Gulf, are harmful because of their potential to spill over from the political and security area into economics and trade. Washington's threat to impose sanctions on European companies investing in the Iranian and Libyan energy sectors led the EU to issue counter-threats against US firms, and to challenge the US in the World Trade Organisation (WTO). A ruling against the US on this issue would undermine American support for the WTO – an organisation critically important to the international trading system. According to senior US and European officials, US sanctions legislation hindered progress in talks on transatlantic trade and investment for more than two years, from 1995–96, when extraterritorial sanctions laws concerning Cuba, Iran and Libya were passed, until May 1998, when the US agreed to waive sanctions on European firms, leading to an at least temporary truce. The stake that European and US leaders have in maintaining open transatlantic trade has kept differences over the Middle East from leading to a trade war or undermining support for the WTO but, until these issues are resolved, the threat to this commercial relationship will persist. Europeans deeply resent – and are determined to resist – the US Congress' use of extraterritorial legislation in the pursuit of foreign-policy goals.

This paper examines the reasons for these potentially damaging differences over the Middle East, assesses the prospects for improving transatlantic cooperation in the region, and suggests approaches that may help to bring this about. There is no simple formula for developing these strategies. Indeed, calls from both sides of the Atlantic for 'better coordination' are often barely concealed demands for the 'other side' to change its policy. Most Americans think that Europe should be more supportive of Israel, accept Washington's diplomatic leadership, maintain sanctions on Iran and Iraq and increase its military contribution in the region. Most Europeans want the US to allow them a role in the peace process, to be more sympathetic to Palestinian aspirations and more flexible towards Iraq, and to lessen its confrontation with Iran.[2] Rather than propose a worthwhile but improbable 'grand bargain' for the Middle East, the main prescriptive aim of this paper is to suggest realistic approaches that may help not only to narrow transatlantic differences over some issues but also, more importantly, to ensure that common US and European interests in the region are realised. This paper's main policy conclusions are:

- On the Middle East peace process, Europe can play a valuable role in financing cooperation among the regional parties, in making certain Arab–Israeli agreements more tenable and in providing a model for cooperation among former enemies. The predominant position of the US in the region, however, means that European attempts to promote outcomes not supported by the US and Israel are likely to be counter-productive, harming transatlantic and Israeli–US relations without bringing peace closer. As long as the peace process is moving forward, Europe's main avenue for influencing it is thus via Washington, by impressing upon US leaders the merits of its views and by adding its diplomatic weight to measures that the US agrees to support. If the US is unable to secure acceptance of its ideas for the region, however, Washington may no longer be able to resist – and may even have an interest in promoting – a more prominent European role.

- On Iraq, given Saddam's record, the US-led policy of containment is necessary, and economic sanctions should remain in place until Baghdad complies fully with UN Security Council resolutions calling for the elimination of its weapons of mass destruction (WMD) programmes. On the other hand, in exchange for Europe's agreement to contribute to Iraq's military containment, the US – like Europe – should be willing to abide by the letter and spirit of these resolutions, even if this means agreeing to lift restrictions on Iraqi oil exports if Baghdad complies in full. Failing to do so could undermine global support for the integrity of the UN system, ultimately leaving the US, and perhaps the UK, isolated in maintaining a policy that might not be sustainable in the long term. Europeans could help to persuade the US to offer this 'light at the end of the tunnel' by agreeing more convincingly to maintain pressure on Iraq, including a strict arms embargo and the threat to use military force if necessary, and by increasing their currently inadequate contribution to military containment in the Gulf.

- On Iran, encouraging changes since May 1997 under new President Mohammed Khatami have begun to allow European and US policies to converge. A transatlantic compromise would need to include an agreement by the US not to impose sanctions against European companies doing business with Iran along the lines of the waiver granted by the State Department to the French firm Total in May 1998. In exchange, Europe would need to offer unstinting support in combating terrorism and helping to contain WMD development. The US should also seek agreement with the EU on which aspects of Iranian behaviour *would* justify sanctions or other punitive measures. This kind of transatlantic agreement has so far been elusive because of differing interpretations of what Iran is doing and which policies are most likely to influence it.

Common policies may be easier to achieve as Iranian behaviour continues to change.

The geographical subject of this paper, 'the Middle East', requires definition, not least because of the ambiguity that surrounds the term.[3] While there is no 'right' definition, this paper focuses on two critical subsets of the Middle East: the Arab–Israeli dispute and the Persian Gulf, with a focus on Iran and Iraq.[4] These two issues are among the most important to Europe and the US in political, economic and strategic terms; they also cause the greatest transatlantic differences. This focus is also appropriate because the politics of the Arab–Israeli dispute and the Persian Gulf interact. Washington's close alignment with Israel, for example, is one of the factors leading the US to take a harder line than Europe towards Iran and Iraq. It has also at times made it more difficult for the US to gather support elsewhere in the Gulf for its policies. Similarly, Europe's greater dependence on oil and gas imports from the Gulf, and its greater vulnerability to instability in the Arab world, has often affected its perspectives on, and policies towards, the Arab–Israeli dispute.

The interrelationship between these two issues is also an important component of the subject of transatlantic policies towards the Middle East because Americans and Europeans tend to disagree on its significance, and on the policy conclusions that should be drawn from it. The US acknowledged a link between the two issues most readily in the 1950s and 1960s, when it tempered its support for Israel in part for fear of alienating the wider Arab world, and the oil-producing Gulf states in particular. The US has also acknowledged a link between the peace process and the Gulf at key moments such as the 1990–91 Gulf War. To ensure continued Arab participation in the coalition against Iraq, Washington did its utmost to persuade Israel not to take part in the fighting, even while Iraqi *Scud* missiles were falling near Tel Aviv. Generally, however, the US downplays the importance of the relationship between the peace process and the Gulf and, at least since the 1970s, has insisted that it can maintain good relations with Israelis and Gulf Arabs alike. Europeans tend to emphasise the importance of the link between the two regions, and draw different policy conclusions from it. They stress that unconditional US support for Israel undermines the West's broader strategic interests in the wider Middle East, and makes it harder for the US to garner Arab support for important strategic goals such as Iraq's containment. Because of these regional linkages, and the US–European differences over their interpretation, this paper considers both sub-regions of the wider Middle East.

Finally, it is necessary to clarify the definitions of the two 'actors' in this analysis, 'the US' and 'Europe'. Both terms imply a unity of purpose and policy that does not, in fact, exist. It is often convenient to refer to 'American' policies and attitudes towards the Middle East, but this generalisation masks essential differences among Congress, public opinion, the administration, the business community and political pressure groups, each of which contains its own internal diversity. These differences are exacerbated by the structure of the US government, which gives Congress, whose policy preferences often differ from those of the administration, powerful leverage over foreign policy, not least in its ability to control spending, impose sanctions, ratify treaties and confirm or reject appointments of senior foreign-policy officials. The term 'Europe' is more misleading still. It can sometimes refer to the EU; sometimes to the main European players in the Middle East such as France, Germany and the UK; and sometimes to a majority of European citizens. In some cases, for example when French and British attitudes and policies diverge considerably, as on Iraq, the concept of 'Europe in the Middle East' is simply a misnomer. This paper is therefore precise in its use of terms, and makes the important distinctions between various actors in the US and European systems. At the same time, however, it sometimes suggests that there are 'US' or 'European' policies and perspectives, since one of the interesting aspects of this subject is the frequency with which differences in policy and analysis run along US–European lines. As much as any debate within the Atlantic Alliance – over NATO enlargement, nuclear weapons, even the former Yugoslavia – there are distinctively 'American' and 'European' views on the Middle East.

chapter 1

Europe's Growing Assertiveness in the Peace Process

Since the late 1960s, two main features have characterised US and European roles in the Arab–Israeli dispute. The first is the pre-eminence of the US in regional diplomacy. Through its global superpower status, military strength, close ties with Israel and huge amounts of economic and military aid to key regional powers, the US has been the privileged interlocutor of all parties in the region. Even most Arab leaders have agreed with the late Egyptian President Anwar Sadat's famous suggestion that the US held '99 percent of the cards'.[1] If the US has had a rival for influence over the Middle East since the 1960s, it was not Europe but the Soviet Union, whose exclusion from the region was a primary US goal throughout the Cold War. When Moscow's global influence declined in the 1980s, and the Soviet Union itself disintegrated in 1991, the US was left as the unrivalled outside power in Middle Eastern politics, with Europe playing a limited, and in many ways subordinate, role.

The second main feature of US and European involvement in the Arab–Israeli conflict has been the US alignment with Israel, while the Europeans took a position closer to that of the Arab states. While often critical of Israeli government policies and, at times, willing to exercise diplomatic or economic leverage over the government, Washington's backing for Israel in its conflict with its Arab neighbours has been unambiguous. The US has provided Israel with unparalleled amounts of economic and military aid, helped to ensure its military superiority over its neighbours and to protect it with military assistance during wartime, and excused or defended its behaviour when it violated international norms, laws, or UN Security Council resolutions. Most Europeans, while firmly committed to Israel's existence, have been more sympathetic to Arab and Palestinian positions, more critical of Israel's occupation of Arab territories captured in 1967 and more willing to maintain normal relations with Israel's regional adversaries.

These two factors are so clear and unquestionable that it is easy to forget how recently each emerged. As colonial states, European nations dominated parts of the Middle East for centuries, and remained influential political, economic and military actors well into the 1960s. Significant US interest in the region did not begin until the Second World War and its aftermath. The Soviet Union's geopolitical and ideological challenge, the growing importance of oil, and the foundation of the State of Israel in 1948 combined to pull Americans out of their traditional parochialism, and led them to rival the Europeans for influence in the Middle East. The US rise to pre-eminence became apparent with the Anglo-French disaster at Suez in 1956. President Dwight D. Eisenhower's administration, furious at what seemed a colonial invasion of an Arab state while the US was competing with the Soviet Union for influence in the developing world, forced London and Paris to back down. Their failure at Suez undermined British and French influence in the region, and helped to establish that of the US.

the US alignment with Israel

Even as it supplanted the Europeans as the leading military and diplomatic player in the Middle East, the US was not in the 1950s the close supporter of Israel that it would become. While Americans had considerable sympathy for Israel, born as it was out of the tragedy of the Holocaust, this was balanced with US interests in Arab oil and sensitivity to alienating Arab states, which might prompt them into aligning with the Soviet Union.[2] As late as the mid-1960s, France (which saw Israel as a useful ally in its struggle against Arab nationalism in Algeria) was Israel's main ally, while the US sought to maintain good relations with the Arab world to the point of refusing to sell weapons to Israel.

With the June 1967 'Six Day War' with Egypt, launched by Israel in response to Egyptian President Gamal Abdel Nasser's closure of the Straits of Tiran the month before, the US alignment with Israel was unambiguously added to its regional pre-eminence as one of the factors that would define the Middle East into the 1990s. Israel's attack on Egypt alienated its main arms supplier, France, which was in any case realigning with the Arab world in the aftermath of its war in Algeria. At the same time, the triumph of tiny, beleaguered Israel over a numerically superior Arab coalition won the country enormous sympathy in the US, where many began to see it as a Cold War asset. Ironically, given French complaints that Israel is today too closely aligned with the US, Paris' arms embargo after the Six Day War helped to drive Israel, ever conscious of the need for a strong external patron, towards Washington. The US has since become Israel's major arms supplier, its closest ally and its defender of last resort.

While the US was aligning itself with Israel, Europe was moving closer to the Arab states. Whereas the October 1973 attack on Israel by Egypt and Syria led the US to adopt a greater role as Israel's protector, Europeans aligned themselves with the Arab side in the conflict, in part for fear of alienating the regimes on whose oil they depended. In November 1973, as part of its early coordination of Middle East policy under the rubric of 'European Political Cooperation', the European Community (EC) acknowledged 'the legitimate rights of the Palestinians' and called on Israel to end its 'territorial occupation' of Arab lands.[3] In the wake of the 1973–74 Organisation of Petroleum Exporting Countries (OPEC) embargo, subsequent economic recession and increased Palestinian terrorism in Europe, the EC developed a 'Euro–Arab' dialogue designed to improve relations with the Arab world and to distinguish the Community's policies from those of the US. These shifts did not, whatever their justification or merit, enhance European influence in the region, particularly with Israel. Americans and Israelis alike would remember Europe's reluctance during the 1973 war to help the US to airlift equipment and supplies that could have been crucial to Israel's survival. Both the US and Israel henceforth sought to limit not only Soviet, but also European, influence in the region.

Europe's most explicit attempt to become involved in the Arab–Israeli peace process during this period, and that which most clearly underlined transatlantic divisions on the issue, was the EC's 'Venice Declaration' of 13 June 1980. While reaffirming Israel's right to exist and to be secure, the Declaration distanced European policy from that of the US by calling for a negotiating role for the Palestine Liberation Organisation (PLO) and by expressing support for the Palestinian people's right to self-determination.[4] The Declaration, which called for an explicit 'political dimension' to EC policy, was a watershed in the Community's attempt to develop as a political and diplomatic actor. It would also, however, contribute to Israeli and US scepticism about Europe's intentions, and thereby to the EC's marginalisation from the peace process. Just three weeks after the Venice Declaration had stated that the EC would 'not accept any unilateral initiative to change the status of Jerusalem', Israel went ahead with East Jerusalem's unilateral annexation, as if to demonstrate that it would pay no heed to European interference. While many Europeans believe that their support for the PLO and Palestinian self-determination has been proved right by later developments, many Israelis and Americans argue that the EC's stance at Venice was premature and showed excessive willingness to meet Arab demands and to take risks with Israeli security. Whether justified or not, this perception led many Israelis and Americans to oppose European involvement in the peace process throughout the 1980s, and it remains a problem in European–Israeli relations.

Europe's exclusion from Middle East peacemaking

The Madrid peace talks in October 1991, organised in the wake of the US-led coalition's victory in the 1991 Gulf War against Iraq, underlined most clearly Europe's exclusion from Middle East peacemaking. For the first time, Israeli representatives met nearly all the country's Arab adversaries in multilateral negotiations. Europe's role, however, was limited to providing the venue for the opening round of talks (the remainder were held in Washington). The official co-sponsors were the US and, despite its rapidly declining influence and impending collapse, the Soviet Union. The Madrid talks were a US-designed plan to take advantage of the Gulf War's aftermath to try to achieve Arab–Israeli peace. The intense pressure the US brought to bear to ensure Israeli participation testified to Washington's unique role in the region. The new peace process also underlined the EC's difficulties in adopting a common approach. The European Commission and the Council squabbled over who should represent the Community at the talks, and Paris objected to allowing the EC presidency to represent France.

While the US dominated Middle East peacemaking in the wake of the Gulf War, Europe suddenly appeared at the centre of events when it emerged in 1993 that Israelis and Palestinians had been conducting secret negotiations under Norwegian auspices in Oslo. These talks led to the 'Declaration of Principles on Palestinian Self-rule' in September 1993. Europeans saw this as a vindication of their approach to the conflict and as underlining the limits of American leadership. While Norway deserved great credit for its mediating role, however, the Oslo approach, which allowed the parties to the conflict to reach agreement with no substantive involvement from the mediating country, was of a different character from the more interventionist style long advocated in the EU. Indeed, for many Israelis, Norway was an acceptable outside mediator only because it was not a member of the Union. It was also telling that the parties to the conflict felt it important that the agreement be signed in Washington and concluded with a handshake on the White House lawn. Subsequent diplomatic negotiations also took place in the US under American auspices. Although Norway offered its good offices and played a crucial honest-broker role, when it came to seeing the peace process through the parties felt that the US was indispensable.[5]

From Convergence to Divergence: Europe Reasserts Itself

The two years following Oslo were marked by an unprecedented convergence of US and European policies towards the peace process. Americans accepted positions long held by Europeans, and Europeans agreed to let the Americans lead. Even if it sometimes grated in European capitals that Washington was taking credit for successes that it had done little to bring about, Europeans did not object to playing a supportive role as long as the Oslo process moved forward. Israeli Prime Minister Yitzhak Rabin and Foreign Minister Shimon Peres were doing what Europe had long advised – recognising the PLO, trading land for peace and moving towards Palestinian self-determination – and the US was facilitating the process. There was thus no need for Europe to interfere. As the Oslo process advanced from the September 1993 Declaration to the March 1994 Cairo Agreements and the Israel–Jordan Peace Treaty of September 1994, transatlantic relations over the Middle East were probably as harmonious as they had ever been. The Israelis were making repeated agreements with their neighbours, the US was acting as the main outside facilitator and honest broker and Europeans were playing an important, if secondary, role.

The cooperation and agreement that characterised Oslo's honeymoon period was not, however, to last. As Arab–Israeli relations began to break down in 1995, so did Europe's tacit agreement to defer to the US, raising old questions about its appropriate role in the peace process, and about whether Europe and the US could agree. By early 1996, European leaders and EU officials were making statements that sometimes differed significantly in tone and content from those of the US. In April 1996, European leaders strongly criticised Israel's *Grapes of Wrath* operation in Lebanon.[6] In October, the EU made its 'Luxembourg Declaration', its most important statement on the Middle East peace process since Venice – and its most critical of Israel.[7] Also in late 1996, several European leaders – French President Jacques Chirac, British Foreign Secretary Malcolm Rifkind, Italian President Oscar Luigi Scalfaro and an EU 'Troika' led by Irish Foreign Minister Dick Spring – visited the region with proposals to move the peace process forward. At the end of October, the EU appointed its own special envoy, Spanish diplomat Miguel Angel Moratinos, to coordinate the European approach to the peace process. Divisions among the Europeans and resistance to the idea in the region meant that the EU was not yet claiming an equal role with the Americans in negotiations. It was nonetheless moving in that direction.[8] As former US Ambassador to Israel Samuel Lewis put it at the time, after having '"passed" on getting involved in the Middle East peace process for about a decade', the Europeans were 'back'.[9]

Europe's renewed efforts to play a role in the region were the result of three main factors. The most important was widespread dissatisfaction with the policies of the Netanyahu government, which took office in May 1996. Even before the election that brought Netanyahu to power, Europeans were critical of the continued growth of Israeli settlements in the West Bank and outraged by the *Grapes of Wrath* operation, which involved widespread bombing of southern Lebanon. They were nonetheless prepared to give Peres, the driving force behind the Oslo agreement and proponent of a 'New Middle East', the benefit of the doubt. Under Netanyahu, however, the peace process broke down, and Europeans laid much of the blame at the Prime Minister's door.[10] The government's decision in September 1996 to open a tunnel near Arab holy places in Jerusalem, the restoration of financial incentives for Israeli settlements in December and the decision in February 1997 to build a new settlement in an East Jerusalem location (called Har Homa by Israelis and Jebel Abu Ghneim by Arabs) were all seen as provocative by Europeans, who were growing frustrated by Washington's inability or reluctance to influence Israel. Many Europeans felt that they could no longer stand aside as they had when Israel had seemed ready to work towards peace, and the US was willing to assist the process. As a French diplomat put it, 'we were quite prepared to defer to the United States so long as it was playing a constructive role and making progress towards peace; but when the US showed itself unwilling to play such a role, Europe decided to get involved'.[11]

A second factor stimulating European involvement in the peace process was Chirac's election to the French presidency in May 1995. Under his predecessor, François Mitterrand, France had been reluctant to play a secondary role to the US, and had been most supportive of an independent EU role in the region. But Chirac's election galvanised French diplomacy. Unable quickly to resolve the social problems that formed a central part of his election campaign, Chirac saw advantages in stressing his country's foreign-policy role, parti-

Europe's renewed efforts to play a role

cularly in the Middle East, which had long been of special interest to France and to Chirac personally.[12] As the President declared during a visit to Qatar in July 1996, 'People have to get used to a return to the presence of France, in particular in this part of the world. We have interests and ideas and are determined to be seen and heard.'[13] Under Chirac, France would repeatedly assert French interests in the Middle East that often contradicted those of the US.

Third, efforts to coordinate foreign policies more generally appear to have prompted some Europeans to play a more active Middle East role. The 1991 Maastricht Treaty called for a Common Foreign and Security Policy (CFSP). By 1996, the CFSP was seen to have enjoyed little success, particularly given Europe's inability to end the war in the former Yugoslavia. When the CFSP came up for review at the EU Intergovernmental Conference (IGC) that began in March 1996, the Middle East peace process seemed a promising area in which to pursue cooperation for three reasons: it was one of the oldest areas of European foreign-policy coordination (dating back to the 'European Political Cooperation' rubric of the early 1970s); it was one of the five priorities identified after Maastricht as a possible area for CFSP 'common positions'; and, relatively at least, it was an area in which Europeans felt that they had similar interests. As one EU official put it, the Union was 'a new player in international relations, so we need visibility and prestige and the Middle East affords us that opportunity'.[14]

These renewed European efforts to play a greater role in the peace process have rekindled an old debate about the appropriate level of European involvement and raised important questions about Europe–US relations in this area. Are the views and interests of the US and Europe sufficiently similar to allow each to play a constructive and cooperative role, or will they inevitably clash? Does Europe have the unity and power to provide an alternative to US leadership, or are Europeans still too weak and divided? Should Europe's role be subordinate to that of the US, or can the CFSP endow the EU with the means to act independently of, or at least be an equal partner with, the US? These questions are taken up in the following chapter.

chapter 2

How and Why the Allies Differ on the Peace Process

Most analysts point out that transatlantic differences over the Middle East should not be inevitable since the basic interests of the US and Europe are broadly the same: peace; regime stability; the free flow of oil; security for an independent Israeli state; a secure homeland for the Palestinians; as much political freedom as possible; and limitations on the spread of WMD.[1] These shared interests clearly distinguish US tensions with Europe from those that characterised the American struggle to reduce Soviet influence in the region. Despite the similarity of basic interests between the US and Europe, however, their policies in the region often differ in a number of respects. To assess the prospects for a convergence of US and European policies, and whether Europe should play a greater role, it is necessary to understand what these differences are, and why they exist.

Policy Differences between the US and Europe

The US tendency to back Israeli positions in the peace process, while Europe tends to support Palestinian goals, is the most basic policy difference between the US and Europe. Americans and Europeans agree on the general principle of 'land for peace' embodied in UN Security Council Resolution 242 of 1967, but differ on how much territory and sovereignty Israel should be asked to transfer to the Palestinians, or at least on how forcefully it should be pressed to do so, in order to reach a just and viable settlement to the conflict. Three particular differences of approach stand out.

1. *The US Emphasises Process; Europe Focuses on Outcomes*

Europe does not hesitate to put forward what it believes to be appropriate elements of a peace package, and often calls for full and immediate Israeli compliance with UN resolutions. The US argues that it is for the parties themselves to decide what would make a stable peace, and that outsiders should limit themselves to providing good offices and acting as honest brokers. Thus, unlike the US, Europeans have been adamant that Israel's occupation of lands acquired in the 1967 war is illegal; that further building of Jewish settlements in the West Bank, or any other measures that would prejudge permanent-status talks, must be stopped; that Israel must withdraw from all of the Golan Heights; and that Israel must abide by UN Security Council Resolution 425 of 1978 calling for it to withdraw from Lebanon without preconditions. The difference between US and European positions on the status of Jerusalem, one of the key stumbling-blocks to a final Israeli–Palestinian settlement, is clearer still. Again, whereas the US takes the view that Jerusalem's future should be decided by agreement between the parties to the conflict, Europeans repeatedly make it clear that they consider Israel's occupation of East Jerusalem illegal and support a Palestinian presence there.[2] Finally, although not all EU member-states formally and officially support eventual statehood for the Palestinians, the EU has moved significantly further in that direction than the US.[3]

On rare occasions, such as in the 1969 Rogers Plan, the 1982 Reagan peace plan, or the Clinton administration's proposals for Israeli 'further redeployments' in the Oslo process in early 1998, the US has offered specific recommendations. The failure of these initiatives, however, has tended to encourage Washington's preference for its traditional approach, which leaves it to the parties themselves to agree on details. According to a prominent American analyst (and as frequently repeated by US officials), 'three core principles' have evolved to guide US peacemaking efforts:

- 'the United States cannot and should not want peace more than the parties themselves;
- the United States cannot impose an agreement on the parties, nor should the United States outline an "American plan" for resolution of the Arab–Israeli dispute; and

- enduring achievements are those made through direct negotiations, with America's principal contribution being to nurture an environment in which the parties themselves could reach accord'.[4]

A high-level 1992 Commission on US–Israel Relations (many of whose members went on to senior foreign-policy positions in the Clinton administration) stated that the 'United States should make clear that a stable and lasting peace is a function of Israeli–Arab agreement, not an agreement imposed by Washington'.[5] Whereas in other parts of the world the US is not shy about putting forward specific plans – the Basic Framework for Peace in Bosnia and Herzegovina (the Dayton Accords) of 1995 is an obvious example – many Americans argue that the most that the US can impose on Israel is a *process*, not a plan. As at Camp David in 1978, this process would give the parties a chance to reach agreement on their own terms.[6]

The American preference for process over specific advocacy is not surprising. Since its main partner in the region, Israel, is the status-quo power, any imposed peace plan would probably mean calling on Israel for concessions that it would not be prepared to make. By not putting forward its own plan, the US is taking the safer route of allowing Israel to determine the pace of the peace process.[7] Unlike Europe, which has long called on Israel to make concessions to which it will not agree, the US is reluctant to push too hard for solutions that it feels may be 'right', but that it believes would nonetheless be rejected. US leaders apparently fear that American credibility as a mediator would quickly be eroded if they found themselves too often making proposals unacceptable to Israel. Washington, particularly under a Democratic presidency drawing heavily on the American Jewish community's support, is unwilling to risk a major, sustained crisis in US–Israeli relations. It therefore shies away from proposing specific plans.

2. US Reluctance to Pressure Israel

Despite having little practical leverage, Europeans often argue that more diplomatic and economic pressure should be exerted on Israel to be more accommodating in the peace process. Although it has never called for economic sanctions to be applied in pursuit of this goal, the EU has occasionally tried to use trading inducements and disincentives in a bid to prompt Israel to change its policies. The European Commission threatened in January 1998 to cut off economic support to the Palestinians if Israel did not stop blockading the Palestinian economy in retaliation for terrorist incidents. The move was perhaps a sign that economic pressure will grow if the peace process deteriorates further.[8] Europe is also more willing than the US to apply international diplomatic pressure, most notably through the UN, where Europeans have often supported resolutions critical of Israel only to see them vetoed by the US. In April 1996, the US blocked an attempt at the Security Council to pass a resolution criticising Israel for its *Grapes of Wrath* operation; in March 1997, the US twice vetoed resolutions critical of the Israeli housing project at Har Homa in East Jerusalem. In this instance, Bill Richardson, the US Ambassador to the UN, stated the US position that the UN was not 'an appropriate forum for debating the issues now under negotiation between the parties'.[9]

The US has, of course, occasionally applied pressure, certainly privately, but also in public. It did so in 1974, when Secretary of State Henry Kissinger threatened a 'reassessment' of US policy in a bid to secure Israeli withdrawal from the Sinai peninsula. In 1978, President Jimmy Carter demanded that Israel withdraw the troops that it had sent into Lebanon. The US pressured Israel again after the Gulf War in 1991, when President George Bush and Secretary of State James Baker publicly lobbied Prime Minister Yitzhak Shamir to attend the Madrid conference. It is widely accepted that Shamir only appeared as a result of this pressure, although it is also known that he refused to concede anything more important than his presence. More significantly, in 1991–92 the Bush administration withheld $10 billion in loan guarantees – needed by Israel to help settle immigrants from the Soviet Union – as a means of pressuring the government to curb its expansion of settlements in the West Bank. The Clinton administration, aware of the political price paid by its predecessors in each of these cases, has strongly favoured the more typical American approach of avoiding public confrontation with Israel. It claims that pressure only incites a negative reaction to perceived 'bullying' – a 'Masada complex', in the words of some

Israel's 'Masada complex'

senior administration officials. Clinton explained his approach in
October 1996:

> *What the United States has done since I have been President*
> *is not to pressure anyone, but to get the parties together and*
> *to explore alternatives and to see what could be done to find*
> *common interests and shared values … Our role is to try to*
> *help bring people together and create the conditions in which*
> *a successful resolution of these matters can occur.*[10]

As the Oslo process continued to deteriorate in 1997 and early 1998,
the US seemed to edge closer to pressuring Israel publicly. In June
1997, Secretary of State Madeleine Albright started calling for a
moratorium on Israeli settlement activities and, in January 1998, the
US began to urge Israel to put forward a 'credible' plan for one of the
'further redeployments' of Israeli forces from the West Bank called
for in the Oslo agreement.

When these calls were not heeded, Washington insisted that
Israel accept, by a proposed deadline of 11 May 1998, a US-drafted
compromise proposal under which Israel would gradually withdraw
from a reported 13.1% of the West Bank. In exchange, the Palestinians
would renew their commitments on fighting terrorism and agree to
move directly thereafter to final-status talks. Despite US threats to 're-
examine' its approach to the peace process if Israel failed to meet the
deadline, Netanyahu ostentatiously refused to accept the proposal.
The administration continued nonetheless to avoid bringing
pressure to bear publicly; Clinton repeatedly stressed that he would
not use the word to describe US policy towards Israel.[11] Even after
Israel's refusal to accept the American proposal or to meet the US
deadline, Clinton stressed that 'There is no way in the world that I
could impose an agreement on them or dictate their security to
them, even if I wished to do that, which I don't.'[12] In the wake of the
Israeli rebuff, many Europeans felt that, as one official put it, 'there
should have been a firm Washington reaction', but it was clear that
the US was unwilling to adopt a more coercive approach.[13]

3. Europe's Economic Focus; America's Military Focus
Security is the primary focus of US policy in the region. The key tool
for achieving it is military assistance and power, areas in which the

US has a comparative advantage over the Europeans. The US provides Israel with $3bn-worth of military and economic assistance annually, and has awarded Egypt more than $2bn each year since Camp David because of Cairo's willingness to make peace and to help ensure the country's domestic stability.[14] Even the $1.2bn in 'economic' aid the US provides Israel with is primarily security assistance since it is used to repay military debts incurred during the Camp David period.[15] Washington also helps to ensure Israel's qualitative military superiority in the region through generous technology transfers and sales of high-technology military equipment. In early 1998, Israel began to take delivery from the US of 25 F-15I fighter aircraft, the most capable fighter-bombers in the US arsenal. Substantial US military assets in the region, including the Sixth Fleet in the Mediterranean, ensure that the US is able, if necessary, to help to defend Israel against its quantitatively superior adversaries.

Europe, on the other hand, pursues its main goals – overall political stability and friendly relations with regional states – with primarily economic means, its own area of comparative advantage. The 'Euro-Mediterranean Partnership', a political and economic relationship between the EU and the states of the Mediterranean littoral, provides long-term EU financial assistance to partner countries ($6.5bn between 1995 and 1999), and emphasises the goal of free trade among its participants. Europe's direct involvement in the Middle East peace process is also primarily economic. Since the Washington donors' conference of 1993, the EU has contributed some 54% of all aid funding to the Palestinian Authority (PA), amounting to some $1.5bn, compared to $280 million from the US.[16] The EU also pays a large proportion of the PA's administrative costs, including the salaries of officials, police and security forces and teachers. Europe is not completely disengaged from issues of military security in the region: since 1995, Europeans have set up several new forces, including EUROFOR, a 15,000-strong arrangement of French, Italian, Spanish and Portuguese troops headquartered in Italy; and EUROMARFOR, a naval grouping comprising the same countries. These forces are, however, primarily conceived with the Western Mediterranean in mind, and are unlikely to play a prominent role in the Middle East.

Why do the US and Europe Disagree?

Why do allies with shared values and broadly common interests disagree on Arab–Israeli issues? Four main reasons help to explain their different approaches to the peace process.

1. Historical Perceptions of Israel and the Arab World

Differing American and European historical relationships with the Middle East have led to differing perceptions of the Arab–Israeli conflict. The close US–Israeli relationship stems from a range of factors, including a shared self-image as new, immigrant-absorbing frontier societies; cultural affinity due in part to the extensive links between Israeli and American citizens; widespread American sympathy for the Jewish people in the wake of the Holocaust; the emphasis in US foreign policy on the democratic values and free enterprise that prevail in Israeli society; and the role of the active and influential US Jewish community. American sympathy for Israel – fostered by relative energy security, Arab alignment with the Soviet Union during the Cold War, distaste for Palestinian terrorism and successful efforts by domestic lobbying groups to portray Israel favourably – grew in the 1960s and 1970s to the point where support for Israel was widespread throughout the country.

Although Europe's main players in the Middle East have also been influenced by some of these factors, they tend to see the region through a different historical lens. From a British perspective, and in particular for much of the British élite, Israel was one of the factors that upset the UK's strategic hold over the region after 1945, rather than a heroic democracy helping the West during the Cold War. Attempts to defy, sometimes with violence, London's restrictions on Jewish immigration to the region led to mutual recriminations, the effects of which remain to this day. France – as the former Mandate power over what is today Lebanon and Syria, and with sensitive relations with its former Arab colonies in North Africa – also tends to see the regional conflict as much through Arab as Israeli eyes. These historically derived perceptions are passed down to successive generations in part through the media. The contrast between the American and European press provides a striking indicator of the general differences in transatlantic perceptions.

2. Differing Domestic Politics

The role of pro-Israeli lobbying groups in the US, and their relative weakness in Europe, is another important factor. The high level of voter participation and political organisation among US Jews sympathetic to Israel makes it difficult for administrations or legislators to take positions that might be perceived as anti-Israeli, let alone to put pressure on Israel to change its policies. This interest-group leverage is increased by the US political system, in which Congress wields significant power over foreign policy, especially where government expenditure is concerned. Since groups like the America–Israel Public Affairs Committee (AIPAC) became powerful in the 1970s, US leaders, particularly Members of Congress, where lobbying groups are especially effective, have been more sensitive to Israeli than to Arab interests. AIPAC, founded in 1951, reportedly has more than 55,000 members and an annual budget of $14.2m.[17] The rising political influence in the US of Christian fundamentalists – many of whom are more staunchly 'pro-Israel' than US Jewish organisations – makes it even more difficult for US politicians to consider policies that Israel opposes.[18] In Europe, where Jewish and other pro-Israeli organisations are less numerous and less influential, no comparable lobbying pressure exists; if anything, Europe's large Arab population creates a channel for dissent against policies seen as too supportive of Israel. As long as stronger domestic political support for Israel persists in the US, America will be more sensitive than Europe to Israel's political and security needs.

3. Europe's Proximity and Vulnerabilities

Differing transatlantic approaches to the Arab–Israeli dispute are also the result of Europe's geographical proximity to the region, which leaves it more vulnerable than the US to immigration, terrorism and threats from missiles and WMD. Europe was most often the venue for Palestinian terrorism at its peak during the 1970s, leading most continental European governments to be particularly cautious about how their policies might be perceived by more radical elements in the Arab world. The US is more physically isolated and secure than Europe, and therefore feels freer to pursue policies that might be perceived as 'anti-Arab' in parts of the Middle East.

Europe is also more dependent than the US on imported Middle Eastern energy. The OPEC oil boycott and price rises of the 1970s were significant factors in Europe's original 'tilt' towards the Arab world. European countries, with the important exceptions of the UK and Norway, which have their own oil reserves, depend on imported supplies for nearly 50% of their energy needs, compared to less than 20% for the US.[19] In addition, a much greater share of Europe's imported energy comes from the Middle East: nearly 60% of Western Europe's oil imports come from the Middle East and North Africa, compared to only 20% for the US.[20] Although oil is a fungible commodity and sources can eventually be diversified, Europe's greater overall dependence on imported energy supplies gives it a particular interest in ensuring the Arab world's stability, and in avoiding its hostility.

4. US Strategic Interests in Israel

If, because of their interest in good relations with Arab countries, Europeans have seen strategic cooperation with Israel as a potential liability, some Americans view the country as a strategic asset. This first struck Americans after the 1967 war, when Israel demonstrated its military and technological prowess by defeating a wide coalition of much larger Arab armies, and both capturing numerous Soviet-made weapons and demonstrating their qualitative inferiority to Western arms. By the 1980s, with Israel's economy continuing to grow far faster than those of its neighbours and its military prominence becoming more marked, many Americans, *some Americans view Israel as a strategic asset* notably the Reagan administration's 'Cold Warriors', welcomed an alliance, particularly with the only stable democracy in the region. While the 'strategic-asset' argument in favour of US support for Israel has become significantly less persuasive with the end of the Cold War, Israel is still seen as a potentially useful strategic partner because of its role in combating opponents of US interests and influence in the region such as Iraq, Iran, Libya and Syria. US strategists, moreover, have begun to think about ways in which military cooperation might be useful in future Gulf military operations if the diminishing of the Arab–Israeli conflict permits more explicit Israeli involvement. The use of Israeli airspace, bases and equipment, as well as Israeli technology transfers to friendly Gulf states (similar to current Israel–Turkey cooperation), intelligence-sharing and pre-positioning facilities in Israel, are all seen as potentially valuable contributions in any future conflict in the Gulf.[21] It is now known that, during the 1991 Gulf War, Israel secretly supplied essential landmine-clearing equipment not only to US forces, but also to Saudi and other Arab troops participating in the US-led coalition.[22] Even if unable to play an open military role as a Western ally, Israel's intelligence on anti-Western regimes in the Middle East, its willingness to cooperate militarily with Turkey, another important US ally in the region, and its ability to undertake military missions that the US could not, such as bombing Iraq's nuclear reactor at Osirak in 1980, lead many Americans to continue to welcome US–Israeli strategic cooperation.[23] Most Europeans, less focused than Americans on global strategic issues or persuaded by the need to 'contain' Iran, Libya and Iraq, believe that the costs of strategic cooperation with Israel outweigh the benefits.

Europe's Own Divisions

The discussion above compares 'European' interests and policies with 'American' ones. There are, however, many different European positions, which is itself one of the constraints on Europe's ability to play a greater role in the peace process. In theory, Europe has sufficient size, wealth, military potential and interest in the peace process to be as powerful an outside actor as the US. What it lacks, however, is the unity and authority of a single nation-state. When an American envoy arrives in the region to cajole the parties, he or she can speak for, and wield the authority of, the US presidency, however constrained by Congress and other factors that may be. An EU envoy, on the other hand, represents 15 nations of varying weight, with different perspectives and sometimes divergent goals. Until this changes, Europe will be a less influential actor than the US.

Like the differences between the US and Europe, the differences among European countries stem from their locations, cultures and historical roles in the region. The UK has intimate personal and commercial ties with Jordan, Saudi Arabia, Kuwait and Oman and, unlike most of its European partners, does not depend on imported oil. France feels a particular affinity with, and responsibility for, its former possession Lebanon, with its Christian minority, and sympathy for Iraq, where it long supported the secular *Ba'athist* regime. Its delicate relations with the Arab countries of the Maghreb incline it towards support for the Palestinian cause. Italy has a special trading relationship with Libya, from which it receives much of its oil, and is particularly vulnerable to refugees and immigration from the Arab world. Germany and Iran have cultural and trading relationships dating back to the nineteenth century, while Germany and Israel have a particular relationship resulting from the Holocaust. The Netherlands has close historical ties with Israel, which it has long supported more strongly than have its European partners. Greece, because of its close links with all of the Arab world, has a particularly troubled relationship with Israel, complicated further by Israel's increasingly close strategic relationship with Greece's historical adversary, Turkey. As a result of these complex interconnections, European countries such as France, Greece and Spain are more determined in their support for a European 'tilt' towards Arab and Palestinian positions; others, including Germany and the Netherlands, are usually closer to Israeli and American views. Still others, including the UK, find themselves sympathetic to Palestinian positions, but reluctant to distance themselves too much from the US. These differences hamper the EU's ability to formulate consistent policies.

European states also have different views of the extent to which their policies towards the Middle East peace process should be channelled through the EU. The UK resists the idea that the Union should be primarily responsible for foreign policy, including in the Middle East. The British are wary of any EU foreign policy too heavily influenced by France, particularly if this were to prompt the Union to distance itself from the US. Germany by contrast seeks to direct virtually all its influence over the peace process through a European channel. Unable, for historical reasons, to take any action that might be perceived as anti-Israeli, Germany has found EU coordination of Middle East policy useful in its efforts to win Arab support. By allowing the EU to take the lead, Germany can pursue both a national special relationship with Israel, and a pro-Arab policy.[24] Since they have little influence of their own, the smaller EU states also generally support a leading EU role in coordinating Middle East policy.

The French attitude towards a leading EU role in European Middle East policy lies between the British and German positions. It is marked by an internal tension between strong European feelings and an enduring desire to play an independent role on the world stage. On the one hand, France is a leading proponent of an EU role in foreign policy in general, and in the Middle East in particular. Paris pushed most strongly for the appointment of an EU envoy to the peace process in 1996, and lobbied most heavily – against British and German resistance – for that envoy to be given a significant role.[25] France has consistently sought to enhance the EU's status as a mediator in the Arab–Israeli dispute, and is one of the few European states formally to support an equal role for the EU alongside the US. As Chirac put it in Damascus on 20 October 1996, 'France and Europe must be present beside the parties – as friends, as a force for proposals, and not just as partners for reconstruction. It is time for Europe to co-sponsor this process as well'.[26] More generally, France has led calls for the EU to develop its CFSP; French proposals at the Union's 1996–97 IGC, including increased majority voting and creating a special representative for European foreign policy, were among the most far-reaching of all the EU states.[27]

While theoretically supporting an EU-led foreign policy in the Middle East, France is reluctant to give up its traditional *national* role. When Israel launched its *Grapes of Wrath* operation in April 1996, Paris did not hesitate to dispatch its Foreign Minister, Hervé de Charette, to the region. The visit was explicitly criticised by Italy, which held the EU's rotating presidency at the time.[28] France pushed for, and received, a seat on the Monitoring Group set up to observe the arrangements between Israel and *Hizbollah* fighters in southern Lebanon. The possibility of a 'European', rather than French, presence in the Group was not supported by Paris and was never discussed. Similarly, in the name of France's newly relaunched Arab policy, Chirac felt free to travel to the Middle East in October 1996 and to articulate positions that were neither coordinated with, nor backed by, other EU member-states. These included support for creating a Palestinian state and an equal role for the EU in sponsoring the peace process.[29] Unless the EU formally adopts a binding foreign and security policy, France is, of course, free to

differences between France and its European partners

follow whichever policies it believes are in its own interests, and those of the region. Doing so, however, is difficult to reconcile with the ultimate objective of a common EU policy as long as all of France's allies do not share all of its views.

Arguably the most significant difference between France and its European partners concerns Europe's particular relationship with the US in Middle East diplomacy. Whereas France formally supports equality for Europe alongside the US, most of its partners believe that Europe should be content with a supporting role. German Foreign Minister Klaus Kinkel argued in 1995 that

> *We [Europeans] do not aspire to a great political role in this regard; namely, the role of a broker, but we want to give advice on this and the other tracks. I tell you that we realise that the Arabs want us to play a more effective role in this regard, but I say that we should leave the political mediation to the Americans, and we, the Europeans, should concentrate further on the economic aid.*[30]

Both British Foreign Minister Rifkind and his Irish counterpart Spring, whose country held the EU presidency at the time, distanced themselves from Chirac's position when he called for greater European involvement in peace negotiations while in the region in 1996. Rifkind stressed that 'The EU wants to complement America's work, not compete with it.'[31] The European Commission is closer to the French position, and in January 1998 called for greater EU involvement in 'all fora set up to assist bilateral negotiations between the parties'.[32] The long-time director of the Commission's Middle East Department, Eberhard Rhein, has, however, expressed a more sceptical view, writing that 'the EU is not up to its political ambition. Realistically, it has to be content with accompanying and complementing US-led initiatives'.[33]

The EU's difficulties in forging a common and effective Middle East policy are primarily the result of the differing views and interests of its most important member-states. These problems are exacerbated, however, by the inability of the EU's institutional foreign-policy structures to forge a common approach where one does not naturally exist. Only if Europe were willing, along the lines of a single state, to delegate genuine authority for Middle East policy to a single executive, backed by a single legislature with power, would it be able to increase its leverage and credibility.

One of the drawbacks of the current EU foreign-policy arrangement is the 'Troika' system, whereby the EU is represented by the current holder of the presidency, along with its immediate predecessor and successor. Among the many disadvantages of this system is the risk that, at times, no major country is represented in international crises. When Iraq invaded Kuwait, the Troika comprised Ireland, Italy and Luxembourg, and was snubbed as irrelevant by Iraq. During the April 1996 crisis in south Lebanon, the Troika consisted of Italy, Spain and Ireland, the first two of which were operating under caretaker governments, while the last had virtually no interests, experience or influence in the region. Without diminishing the contribution of the able diplomats in the small European countries, the credibility, continuity and unity necessary to represent, let alone make, EU foreign policy effectively does not exist under the current system.[34] New arrangements agreed at the June 1997 Amsterdam IGC would supplement the holder of the EU presidency with a newly created High Representative for foreign policy and the Vice-President of the EU Commission. This may help to provide more continuity in foreign policy, but is unlikely to solve the problem of the lack of representation for the EU's larger and more influential states.

The position of High Representative agreed at Amsterdam also raises questions over what sort of relationship its incumbent will have with the EU's envoy to the peace process. The Union has been reluctant to appoint a high-profile politician to either position, or to endow either with significant authority (both are limited to coordination and representation). This raises doubts over member-states' commitment to transferring further authority to the EU where foreign – and Middle East – policymaking is concerned. NATO has traditionally appointed as its Secretary-General former Foreign or Defence Ministers with close contacts throughout the Alliance and with significant influence (Javier Solana, Manfred Wörner and Lord Carrington, for example). The EU by contrast seems unwilling or unable to agree on a more unified institutional structure, and has left responsibility for the Middle East divided between several unelected Commissioners; a High Representative who may not be a prominent political figure; a special envoy restricted to reporting and informing, rather than shaping, policy; and 15 Foreign Ministers, some of whom have their own national agendas and interests. This makes it difficult for the EU to frame a unified, and therefore more influential, approach. These compromises and institutional divisions may be inevitable, but they need to be acknowledged.

Should Europe Play a Greater Role?

With the peace process at an impasse, many Europeans are starting to take the view that Europe should not be as passive a partner of the US as it was when the Oslo process was moving forward more successfully. Although most Europeans do not share the argument, made by both France and the Commission, that Europe should become a formal co-sponsor of bilateral talks in the peace process, few disagree with British analyst Rosemary Hollis' argument that 'Europe qualifies for a much more significant role in the Middle East than it is currently accorded'.[35] Given Europe's stake in regional security, its financial contributions to one of the parties to the conflict and the apparent inability of the US to bring peace on its own, Europe has begun to claim a greater role.

Few Americans, however, are ready to accept Europe as a full partner in the Middle East. Most US officials, as Richard Haass has noted, 'tend to view European statements and actions affecting the peace process as "meddling" that only complicates the already difficult task of promoting political progress among the local parties'.[36] Many Americans go further, sharing Robert Satloff's argument that 'By its actions and positions, Europe has disqualified itself from the broker/sponsor role.'[37] As Mortimer Zuckerman and Lester Pollack have put it in rejecting calls for Europe to be more involved, 'the United States for decades has sought to limit the involvement of others, including Russia and the Europeans, in the Middle East peace process. To involve the Europeans at this stage, in a new dialogue, would seem to be as counterproductive in the future as it has been in the past'.[38] The fact that even those Americans most supportive of a greater European role assume that the US must remain the partnership's clear leader testifies to the limits of what the US might be prepared to accept in terms of Europe's involvement in the peace process.[39]

Should Europe play a greater role? While it will be difficult for the US to involve Europe in the peace process more than it feels it must – great powers rarely consciously share their authority without being obliged to do so – there are ways in which Europe's role in the region could be in the US interest. Without giving up leadership of the process, Washington should take advantage of, rather than oppose, Europe's willingness to devote attention and resources to the search for Middle East peace.

First, even short of a major military contribution to security, which is unlikely, the EU plays a crucial financial role that will be all the more important if further peace agreements are reached. The US has so far managed to maintain financial transfers to Egypt and Israel of more than $5bn a year, but foreign-aid budgets are under pressure and the US cannot bankroll Middle East peace alone. Financial aid and trade are limited but useful tools in both the Middle East peace process and the Gulf. Were the US and the EU to work towards common aims, the impact of their joint market of nearly 600m people and $13 trillion could be decisive. European financial support will almost certainly be needed should further peace agreements be reached between Israel and its neighbours. It should not be forgotten that the more than $5bn allocated yearly by the US to bolster the Israel–Egypt peace treaty totals some $100bn in the two decades since the agreement was reached. If Israel nears agreement with Syria or Lebanon, a critical final ingredient might be an outside offer of funding for the parties – to ensure their access to clean water; provide work for demobilised troops and help with military restructuring; resettle refugees; and aid in the transition to a more liberal economy. Europeans are likely to help to fund any peace agreement, but the US might be better placed to persuade them to play a greater role in this area if full consultation begins before the final bill arrives.

few Americans accept Europe as a full partner

Second, ensuring Europe's association with certain diplomatic agreements could help to contribute to their viability. Increasingly, especially as the Arab–Israeli peace process has broken down, the US is perceived in much of the Arab world as strongly biased towards Israel, and unwilling to play an honest-broker role. As a result, deals put forward by the US without Europe's support may be more difficult for Arab regimes to accept, lest they become subject to domestic accusations of giving in to a US–Israel coalition. The

Europeans, on the other hand, with their long record of support for the Palestinian cause and relatively less antagonism with regional powers like Syria or Iran, may be able to make certain deals more acceptable to the regional partners. European involvement in a peacekeeping force on the Golan Heights, a truce-monitoring arrangement in Lebanon, an Israeli–Palestinian territorial compromise, election monitoring, a plan for a code of conduct among Palestinians and Israelis, or an enhanced inspection regime of regional nuclear facilities could make the difference between what is acceptable to Arab countries and what is not. If a Palestinian state is to be demilitarised, outside involvement will be crucial, and a European role may be more acceptable to Palestinians – and to Americans, for that matter – than US involvement alone. Israel's appeal to France in February 1998 to explore possible arrangements that would allow it to withdraw its troops from Lebanon is an example of the kind of role Europeans might be able to play.[40]

A third contribution Europe can make to Middle East peace is as a model of what former enemies can achieve. This is less tangible, but still important. In a dialogue with Israelis and Arabs, the Germans and French can speak with some authority about the possibility of overcoming so-called 'hereditary conflict'. It would be naive to think that, simply by force of example, EU states could show Middle Eastern countries the way towards cooperation, integration and even federation. Hopes for a 'New Middle East' along the lines proposed by former Israeli Prime Minister Peres have proven premature. Nonetheless, the EU is a remarkable demonstration that resolving ethnic, border and religious disputes is both possible and beneficial. Moderate Middle Eastern leaders could learn much from their European counterparts about how to build cooperation out of conflict.

Do these factors qualify Europe for a 'much more significant role', as Hollis argues? As long as the peace process is moving forward, or has reasonable prospects of doing so, the US is probably right in its view that a formal role for Europe in direct peace talks would not be helpful, particularly if such a role aimed to promote policies different from those of the US. If, as a formal co-sponsor of the peace process, 'Europe' sought outcomes that, however 'just', would be opposed by the US, the European role would be likely to contribute more to transatlantic recrimination and tension than to regional peace. Palestinian and Israeli negotiators could play their respective sponsors off against each other, each side holding out for a better deal in the hope that their sponsor would support them. If, on the other hand, the peace process stalls completely, and the US is unable to secure Israeli acceptance of even its most accommodating suggestions for progress, it will be difficult for Washington to oppose greater European activism. With nothing to show for its mediation efforts, the US would have little basis to block – and might even want to support – proposals like the May 1998 Franco-Egyptian idea for a new international conference of 'countries determined to save the peace'.[41] If a frustrated US government ever decides publicly to put forward specific peace proposals, and determinedly pressures both Israel and the Palestinians to accept and implement them, greater European involvement in a common front would be useful. The best arrangement for the peace process remains one in which the US is the sole formal mediator, and the parties accept its proposals. If this arrangement is seen to fail, however, it will be difficult for Washington to justify opposing Europe's more active involvement.

Can the US–European Gaps be Bridged?

The US and Europe have a history of disagreement over policy towards the Arab–Israeli conflict, and these disagreements have deepened since the peace process stalled. This discussion does not mean, however, that post-Oslo developments necessarily mark a permanent trend, and that efforts to bring American and European policy closer are futile. The enduring differences among the Atlantic allies should not be denied, but there are several reasons to believe that they can be overcome.

First, while there are significant transatlantic divisions, the US and Europe share fundamental aims: both seek a settlement of regional issues that includes an independent and secure Israel, a homeland for the Palestinians and mutual recognition between Arab states and Israel. The US and Europe have agreed on policy towards the Arab–Israeli conflict in the past – in the early 1960s, for example, and as recently as the early 1990s – and they can do so again. It is important not to allow the problems of 1996–98 to obscure the long-term importance of the positive changes that have taken place since 1993. Israelis, for the first time since the advent of *Likud*-led governments in the late 1970s, accept the principle of land for peace, a prerequisite not only for a settlement between Israelis and Palestinians, but also for agreement between Americans and Europeans. *Likud*'s 1996 election campaign was the party's first not to stress 'Greater Israel' as a major theme, and the Netanyahu government, notwithstanding its hardline stance and criticism of its predecessors' policies, has accepted the legitimacy of the Oslo agreements and taken the significant step of withdrawing from most of Hebron, Judaism's second most sacred site. It has also begun to accept the idea of an autonomous Palestinian entity, even if not all Israelis are ready to call it a 'state'.[42] As long as Israeli governments clung to the

how transatlantic policies could change

notion that Israel had to retain control of all of the West Bank as part of the Jewish homeland, as was the case throughout most of the 1980s and early 1990s, transatlantic agreement was as unlikely as peace with the Palestinians. By the late 1990s, even some conservative Israeli analysts had accepted, albeit grudgingly, the likelihood that a Palestinian autonomous entity, or even a state, would be created.[43] Significant differences persist among Israelis, and between Americans and Europeans, on the degree of sovereignty and amount of territory a self-determined Palestinian area should have – but not on the principle of whether it should exist. The gaps across both the Green Line separating the West Bank from pre-1967 Israel and across the Atlantic are narrower than they were before the Oslo process began.

Second, convergence between Americans and Europeans could come about if Israel's policies change. It seems clear that the Netanyahu government has been largely responsible for the divergence not only between Arabs and Israelis, but also between the US and Europe. Even if, as Netanyahu and his allies point out, the Prime Minister could not have been expected to give less support to West Bank settlement activity than his Labor predecessors, it is also true that Palestinians and the rest of the Arab world were more willing to accept settlement growth and other policies when the Israeli government was at the same time holding out the inducement of further transfers of territory and sovereignty.[44] An Israeli government that pursues policies more inclined to lead Palestinians to give it the benefit of the doubt is more likely to create the necessary conditions under which US and European approaches towards the peace process can converge.

Finally, transatlantic *rapprochement* is possible because American positions on the peace process may shift. Americans have tended to downplay the link between US policy towards the peace process and wider strategic issues in the Gulf, but this could change if the strategic costs of unconditional support for Israel begin to mount. In late 1997, at least in part due to frustration with Israeli policy towards the peace process, leading Arab regimes took several steps that reminded Americans of the potential costs of a stalemated peace process: they refused to pursue the regional economic cooperation encouraged by the US; began a process of *rapprochement* with Iran that culminated in the well-attended summit of the Organisation of the Islamic Conference (OIC) in Tehran in December (in contrast to the widespread Arab refusal to attend the US-supported Middle East–North Africa (MENA) economic-cooperation summit in Qatar several weeks before); and were reluctant to offer significant support to the US military build-up during the November–December inspections crisis with Iraq. While these events were not all a result of developments in the peace process, it was not a coincidence that, during the same period, the US redoubled its efforts to persuade Israel to accept a moratorium on West Bank settlements and to make further military redeployments called for in the Oslo agreements. The more difficult Israeli policies make it for Arab regimes to associate with the West and the US, the harder it will be for Washington to avoid pressuring Israel to make concessions in negotiations with the Palestinians.

Moreover, it can no longer be assumed that the Jewish community in the US will automatically lobby to prevent American positions on peace-process issues that include significant transfers of sovereignty and territory to Palestinians, and possibly to Syrians and Lebanese, such as those advocated by the Europeans. The US Jewish community is, in the late 1990s, as divided over the peace process as Israel itself. Many American Jews feel that if territorial and functional concessions to Arabs were good enough for a traditional Israeli security hawk like Yitzhak Rabin, they are good enough for them. Public-opinion polls among American Jews show increasing hostility towards the Netanyahu government's policies, and some even indicate that US Jewish groups are willing to support

US pressure on Israel to move the peace process forward.[45] According to journalist Jonathan Broder of *The Jerusalem Report*, an October 1997 dinner hosted by Clinton for leaders of the US Jewish community represented a watershed in its support for a tougher policy towards Israel: 'Never before had the community's top leadership effectively given the administration a green light to apply pressure on Israel to be more forthcoming in peace talks.'[46] Around the same time, and for similar reasons, a Council on Foreign Relations (CFR) study group, which included several leading analysts and former senior officials, came out in favour both of the US presenting a specific peace plan, and of 'far greater co-ordination with its European and regional allies'.[47] The report was controversial, and several members of the group appended dissenting views, but the overall message calling for a change in US policy was potentially important.

Much political opposition to putting pressure on Israel remains: 81 Senators, for example, mobilised in part by AIPAC, signed a letter in April 1998 warning Clinton *not* to pressure Israel, and more than half of the members of the House of Representatives signed a similar letter the following month.[48] Nonetheless, if Israel continues to oppose even limited US pressure for concessions, Washington might finally feel obliged to overcome its reluctance to proposing, and publicly pushing for, a specific peace plan, rather than allowing Israel to go at its own pace. This remains unlikely for the reasons that US administrations have avoided it in the past. However, if the costs of the current policy begin to mount – in terms of regional stability and relations with important Arab states in the Gulf – a US decision publicly to pressure Israel could become more likely than it has been for several years. If the US pursues this course, it could expect Europe to support it.

chapter 3

The Evolution of Transatlantic Divergence in the Gulf

Since the end of the Second World War, Western policy in the Gulf has been characterised by some of the same factors that mark Western policy in the Arab–Israeli dispute: US leadership, especially in the strategic area, with Europeans playing a secondary, essentially economic, role; strong US support for Israel, in this case leading the US to oppose hostile states like Iraq and, after 1979, Iran; and sensitivity to the common Western need for oil and gas from the Gulf. Whereas transatlantic involvement in the Arab–Israeli conflict has been marked by significant and recurrent tensions dating back to the Suez crisis, US and European policies towards the Gulf have tended to be less at odds with each other. US and European firms have been economic competitors, particularly in the arms and energy sectors, but, until the 1990s, the Gulf did not generate the type of transatlantic tensions caused by the Arab–Israeli conflict.

As in the Arab–Israeli dispute, the predominant US role in the Gulf – at the expense of the European powers, particularly the UK – can be traced to the mid-1950s. As the 1950s began, the UK was the leading outside power in the Gulf region. London maintained military protectorates over most of the small Arab Gulf states; played an important role in Iraq, which only gained full independence in 1958; and dominated Iran, where the Anglo-Iranian Oil Company had major interests and enjoyed significant influence. Other European countries played only limited roles in the region, with France's historical influence limited to its former Mandate in Lebanon and Germany excluded from even its erstwhile areas of influence such as Iran because of its role in the Second World War. With the possible exception of the Netherlands through its stake in Royal Dutch Shell, the smaller European states were not heavily involved in the region's politics or diplomacy. The US played a significant role in Saudi Arabia, where the Arabian–American Oil Company (Aramco) had held the main oil concession from 1933, but otherwise it had yet to establish itself as a leading political and military force.

The gradual replacement of British with American hegemony in the Gulf began with the 1951 election in Iran of a nationalist and anti-British Prime Minister, Mohammad Mossadeq, who nationalised Anglo-Iranian after it refused to pay greater compensation to its host country. British oil officials were chased out of the country, and were only to return after August 1953, when the US helped to arrange a coup that restored the Shah, Mohammad Reza Pahlavi, to power. Under the new arrangements, US oil companies were given a stake equal to that of the British, and the US became the primary outside sponsor and military supplier of the Shah's regime. This would have a significant impact on the US role in the region in coming decades.

The 1960s saw a further transfer of influence in the Gulf from London to Washington. As the UK declined as a global economic and military power, it gradually became clear that, if the pro-Western Sheikhdoms of the Gulf were to be supported against internal unrest and/or Soviet interference, the task would fall as much, if not more, to the US than to the UK. By 1968, Britain concluded that it could no longer sustain its deployment of significant military forces 'East of Suez', and by December 1971 most had been withdrawn. The UK maintained extensive contacts and political influence, but henceforth the US would be the major outside power in the region. This would rest on two main pillars: the Shah's Iran and Saudi Arabia. Unlike the Arab–Israeli conflict over Suez, the US replacement of British influence in the Gulf did not cause great tension between London and Washington. As economic constraints forced the British to cut back on their military commitments in the Gulf, they were only too happy to be replaced by a friendly US. Both had common objectives: to ensure a continued flow of oil to the West (an aim that grew more important after the OPEC embargo of 1973–74); and to exclude Soviet influence in the region.

The Iranian revolution of 1979, while a shock to Americans and Europeans alike, set the basis for some of the tensions over the Gulf that would later emerge between the allies. The removal of the US-backed Shah, the seizure of US hostages and the new regime's support for terrorism and opposition to Israel combined to leave a venomous legacy that would mark US–Iranian relations into the 1990s. In addition, by undermining one of the regional pillars on which US influence in the region rested, the revolution led Washington to move closer to Iraq, thereby inadvertently fuelling Saddam's appetite for dominating the region. The debate about how to contain Saddam's aggressive regime would later cause friction between the US and Europe, but at the time Iraqi behaviour provided a further basis for building up a dominant US military presence in the region. The Soviet invasion of Afghanistan, which took place just a month after the seizure of the US Embassy in Tehran, only reinforced the trend. It led the US to issue the 'Carter Doctrine', declaring that an attempt by any outside force to gain control of the Persian Gulf region would be considered an attack on the vital interests of the US.

During the 1980s, the general Western agreement on Gulf policy was evident in the attitudes and policies towards the 'first Gulf War' between Iran and Iraq in 1980–88. While some states such as France were more explicit than others in their 'tilt' towards Iraq during the conflict, Americans and Europeans alike claimed formal neutrality and were relatively disinterested in the war as long as it did not affect shipping in the Gulf. When the flow of oil was affected, as Iraq began targeting the tankers that carried most of Iran's oil out through the Gulf, and Iran responded in kind, the US and European reaction was again a common one. Beginning in July 1987, a number of European allies followed the US lead in providing military escorts for tanker traffic.[1]

The outbreak of the 'second' Gulf War, when Iraq invaded Kuwait in August 1990, only strengthened the general transatlantic consensus on policy in the region. Whatever the different biases and interests of the Americans and Europeans, Iraqi aggression was so blatant that it forced all of the West, and indeed most Arab governments, into the same camp. While nearly all the NATO allies eventually joined the coalition, the various Western reactions to the invasion of Kuwait revealed much about their respective positions.

The Americans and Europeans played to type: the US took the lead, emphasised the need for military action, led the international coalition and provided the overwhelming majority of the forces. The UK lent its immediate and unwavering support, and provided the most significant European military contribution. France, traditionally both less willing to stand unquestioningly by the US and cautious about offending the Arab world, wavered before becoming involved. The eventual deployment of 12,000 troops followed much agonising, the resignation of the Defence Minister, Jean-Pierre Chevènement, and several last-minute attempts to mediate between Iraq and the coalition. Germany, again typically, stood midway between the French and British positions. Constrained by its past and by an interpretation of its Constitution that prevented it from deploying military forces abroad, Bonn strongly supported the US financially, but did not take part in the military coalition. Other European states also acted as expected, supporting US leadership of the coalition politically and providing limited military contributions.[2] This pattern was important because, when another Iraq crisis emerged seven years later over UN arms inspections, US and European reactions would be remarkably similar to those during 1990–91.

From Cooperation to Divergence: Differences over Dual Containment

As in the Middle East peace process, US and European policies in the immediate aftermath of the Gulf War converged. On Iraq, a set of intrusive UN Security Council resolutions outlined the basic policy; in the light of Saddam's recent aggression, there was no argument over the need for strict containment. On Iran, policy differences among the allies were minimal, despite the fact that US relations with Tehran were worse than Europe's. The US had no diplomatic ties with Iran and had, since 1987, maintained a ban on imports from the country. It did not, however, try to prevent European firms from doing business there, and US oil companies remained heavy buyers of Iranian oil on the open market.[3] In late 1992, the US Congress passed the Iran–Iraq Arms Non-Proliferation Act, which foreshadowed later sources of tension by calling for sanctions on even foreign firms or governments helping Iran to develop WMD or 'destabilising numbers' of advanced conventional weapons. The legislation was not particularly controversial. When the Bush administration left office in January 1993, US–European positions in the Gulf, although not identical, were not in conflict either.

The origins of transatlantic divergence on the Gulf date back to the beginning of the first Clinton administration, which took office in January 1993 determined to put in place a new US strategy for the Gulf. Dubbed 'Dual Containment', the new approach was most clearly spelled out in a speech to the Washington Institute for Near East Policy by then National Security Council official Martin Indyk in May 1993.[4] Dual Containment was predicated on the belief that, with no Soviet patron available for either Iraq or Iran; the US in a dominant regional position in the wake of the Gulf War; the Arab–Israeli peace process underway; and both Iraq and Iran weakened by eight years of war and international isolation, the US no longer needed to pursue its traditional policies of balancing either country against the other. Now, for the first time, the US could keep both in check simultaneously. Dual Containment was designed to deter Iraq and Iran from threatening their neighbours (or oil supplies), to prevent them from acquiring WMD, and to stop them from meddling in the Arab–Israeli peace process, a priority for the staunchly pro-Israeli administration.

transatlantic divergence over Iran and Iraq

As initially outlined, Dual Containment did not cause a major policy rift with the Europeans. Although in his Washington Institute speech Indyk referred to Saddam as 'irredeemable', foreshadowing a later dispute with Europe about whether sanctions could be lifted while he remained in power, the new policy contained no sanctions on Iraq that were not already clearly spelled out in UN Security Council resolutions, which all the allies agreed should be implemented in full. On Iran, while Europeans may have disagreed with the tone of some US rhetoric (including use of the word 'containment'), the actual policies of Americans and Europeans were not markedly different. According to Indyk, the US hoped to persuade its European allies to prevent Iran from pursuing 'normal commercial relations' and to take measures to hinder Iranian conventional and nuclear military development. However, Indyk did not call for, nor did he threaten to put in place, any coercive measures to ensure that this was done. Europeans had no reason to doubt that the US was simply restating its preference for a slightly harder line, and there was little cause to suspect that transatlantic relations over the Gulf would in coming years reach as low a point as they ever had before.

This is, however, precisely what took place. On Iraq, by the mid-1990s, the general transatlantic consensus on how to contain the regime started to break down, and some European countries, notably France, began to distance themselves from US policy. They opposed the American stance, made explicit in 1997, of linking the eventual lifting of sanctions to Saddam's removal, and accused Washington of changing the rules and undermining the UN. No one in Europe was as yet arguing for unrestrained dialogue and openness with Saddam, or claiming that Iraq did not pose a potential regional threat. It was clear, however, that the threshold for ending containment was for most Europeans significantly lower than for the US and the UK.

Transatlantic relations also took a turn for the worse over Iran after 1995 and, by 1996, US–European policy differences threatened to spill over into a serious commercial conflict. After the election to Congress of a hardline Republican majority in November 1994, the US began to back up the tough rhetoric of Dual Containment with action. Competition between the administration and Congress over which could be firmer on Iran led to a tougher policy. This competition was fuelled by the side-effects of the deteriorating Israeli–Palestinian relationship. Official Iranian applause for suicide bombings in Israel, along with evidence of the country's military and financial support for *Hizbollah*'s war against Israeli soldiers in southern Lebanon, made US policymakers more determined to isolate and punish Tehran.[5] Israel began to publicise intelligence reports – taken more seriously in Washington than in Europe – claiming that Iran was actively developing nuclear weapons and ballistic missiles. Most Europeans tended to blame the breakdown in Israeli–Palestinian relations primarily on the Netanyahu government's hardline policies, rather than on Iranian interference, and they disagreed with the American attempt to link the two issues in this way. By the end of 1996, the US had not only unilaterally placed a near-total embargo on US trade and investment in Iran, but had also passed laws calling for sanctions against foreign – notably European – firms making large investments in Iran's energy sector.

Europeans denounced these moves as both ill-advised and illegal, and threatened serious counter-measures, including bringing a case against Washington at the WTO.

Why did the US and Europe, traditionally in general agreement about most of these issues, come to such different conclusions on how to deal with Iraq and Iran? Have the mid-1990s simply been an exception to a long period of relative transatlantic harmony on the Gulf, or is this disagreement a sign of a more significant and enduring strategic split? Can the gaps across the Atlantic, and sometimes across the English Channel, be bridged, and what policy approaches are most likely to improve relations? The next chapter looks at the factors that divide the Americans from the Europeans, and often some Europeans from others; seeks to explain the political, economic and cultural reasons for these differences; and outlines strategies most likely to bring about common transatlantic policies to realise shared Euro-American interests in the Gulf.

chapter 4

How and Why the Allies Differ over the Gulf

As in the Arab–Israeli conflict, it is too simple to speak of 'US' and 'European' positions on the Gulf as if the US and Europe were unitary actors. In many cases, particularly on Iraq, there is more that unites the allies than divides them, and the divisions that do exist are sometimes as much among Europeans or Americans, as between the US and its allies. Nonetheless, there are profound US–European differences over important issues concerning the Gulf. It is impossible to assess the prospects for more unified transatlantic policies without understanding the content and sources of this divergence.

Policy Differences in the Gulf

Among the many policy issues that divide the allies, three cases are most important.

1. Conflicting Strategies towards 'Rogue' States

Perhaps the greatest difference between Americans and Europeans in the Gulf concerns the two sides' overall, long-term strategies for dealing with what the US, since 1994, has called 'backlash' or 'rogue' states.[1] Most Europeans argue that, in the long term, dialogue and trade are the best tools with which to gain influence over countries, and that prosperity and interaction are the best ways of spreading democracy and enhancing cooperation. In this view, trade fosters common interests and greater harmony among nations, and stimulates business activity and political change. As Rheinhard

Schlageintweit, the former Director of the German Foreign Ministry's Near and Middle East Section, has put it, 'If the West could ... build up economic, cultural, and political ties [with Iran], it would reply to a great interest in the emerging bourgeoisie, and encourage the gradual opening up of Iran's foreign policy.'[2] Most Europeans are sceptical that US policies of punishment and containment can work, and argue that 'demonising' élites in these so-called rogue states only fuels their determination to resist Western hegemony. This gives them a public excuse for their poor economic and social performance.[3]

The typical American response to Europe's aversion to coercive or punitive measures is to say that it is either cynical – a pretext for pursuing economic relationships – or naive. Americans argue that rogue regimes are probably immune to reform and that, even if it were possible eventually to change them, they would do so much damage in the meantime that the risk of trying is too great. Trade and dialogue with rogue states do not, at least in the short term, foster openness and political change; rather, they give these hostile regimes more resources with which to carry out their destructive programmes and remove any incentive they might have to mend their ways. The US objective is thus to maintain pressure to force these regimes to change, and to keep them from doing much damage in the meantime.[4]

The greater European preference for engagement and positive incentives is clearest on Iran. EU states have consistently favoured dialogue and trade over coercion, despite evidence of Tehran's support for terrorism, violations of human rights, support for violent opposition to the Arab–Israeli peace process and suspected development of a nuclear-weapons programme. Despite these factors, the Europeans have not suspended trade or imposed other economic sanctions. As French Foreign Minister Hubert Védrine put it in 1997, 'The simple idea that one should not have any trade of any kind with states that one complains about or fears for this reason or that is an idea that no responsible government defends.'[5] Even after a German court in April 1997 cited the involvement of senior Iranian officials in a 1992 political murder in the Mykonos restaurant in Berlin, the EU only temporarily withdrew its ambassadors and 'suspended' its 'critical dialogue'. This policy, pursued for the previous five years, sought to influence Iran through diplomatic means.[6] By the end of the year, the EU ambassadors were back in their posts, and Europeans again stressed the need for continued economic and diplomatic engagement. The US, by contrast, has had no diplomatic relations with Iran since 1980, and since 1995 has imposed a wide variety of punitive measures on the regime.

Transatlantic differences over 'engagement versus containment' are less pronounced on Iraq, where most Europeans agree that military containment remains necessary, and where UN Security Council sanctions oblige them to keep economic containment in place. Nonetheless, most of Europe, particularly France, is more willing than the US to envisage engagement with Baghdad. In January 1995, France became the first Western country to break with the post-Gulf War policy of ostracising the Iraqi leadership when it welcomed Iraqi Foreign Minister Tariq Aziz to Paris; by the end of 1997 Spain, Greece and Italy had all reopened Embassies in Baghdad. French and Italian construction and

Europe prefers engagement; the US emphasises coercion

oil companies have been visiting Iraq to position themselves for post-sanctions contracts. Perhaps most tellingly, almost all Europeans strongly disagree with the US view, expressed most clearly in March 1997 by Secretary of State Albright, that economic sanctions on Iraq should remain in place as long as Saddam holds power. Whereas previously US officials had only vaguely suggested that sanctions might be linked to Saddam, Albright seemed to harden the policy by stating that

> We do not agree with the nations who argue that if Iraq complies with its obligations concerning weapons of mass destruction, sanctions should be lifted. Our view, which is unshakeable, is that Iraq must prove its peaceful intentions. It can only do that by complying with all of the Security Council Resolutions to which it is subject. Is it possible to conceive of such a government under Saddam Hussein? ... the evidence is overwhelming that Saddam Hussein's intentions will never be peaceful.[7]

Whereas Americans appear ready to maintain sanctions on Iraq 'as long as it takes', to use Albright's words, Europeans tend to share

Italian Prime Minister Romano Prodi's goal of a 'weakening and then a lifting of the embargo', even if that means dealing with Saddam.[8]

2. The Greater US Emphasis on Military Force

A second significant difference between the US and Europe in the Gulf is Washington's greater reliance on military force. The pro-Western countries in the region – Saudi Arabia, Kuwait and the smaller Gulf states – depend heavily for their defence on US forces, both those in the region, and those earmarked for deployment from the Florida-based US Central Command, created for this purpose in January 1983. Among European countries, the UK has defence agreements with Kuwait and the United Arab Emirates (UAE), France with Kuwait, Qatar and the UAE. Neither country, however, has forces on a scale even approaching those of the US, whose deployment in the region in the mid-1990s included some 20,000 troops, 200 aircraft, 20 ships in regional and adjacent waters (as part of the new Fifth Fleet, created in 1997 and based in Bahrain), and more than $1.2bn-worth of pre-positioned equipment in Saudi Arabia, Kuwait and Qatar.[9] US arms sales to its Gulf allies, which total more than $40bn since the Gulf War, form an integral part of US military policy in the region.[10]

As well as a greater reliance on military force for deterrence, the US is also more willing than Europe to use it. Since the Gulf War, Washington has twice mounted cruise-missile attacks against Iraq: in June 1993 in response to an Iraqi assassination attempt on former President Bush during a visit to Kuwait; and in September 1996, after an Iraqi military incursion against a Kurdish opposition faction in the north of the country. The 1996 strike was widely criticised in Europe, particularly by France; the UK was the only EU member to give it full support. Shortly afterwards, France withdrew from participation in the northern 'no-fly zone' set up in 1991, claiming that it was no longer the humanitarian operation to which Paris had initially agreed, but a military operation without UN authorisation.[11] On several occasions, the US has also quickly deployed military assets to the region. It did so in October 1994, when Iraq moved forces into position to threaten Kuwait, and in October 1997, when Iraqi aircraft challenged the southern no-fly zone. Although the US has not used force against Iran, its policies of Dual Containment, an arms embargo and unilateral economic sanctions, explicitly designed to hamper Iranian military acquisitions, place a heavy emphasis on the need to contain Iran militarily. Most Europeans do not share this view.[12]

The weapons-inspection crisis of late 1997 and early 1998 is possibly most indicative of Washington's greater willingness to use – or at least threaten – force. Saddam's refusal to cooperate with arms inspectors prompted a massive US military build-up in the region in preparation for air-strikes should Iraq remain obdurate. As in the 1991 Gulf War, the UK offered the most immediate and unambiguous support, dispatching significant military assets to the region.[13] But the hesitant reaction of other European countries belied British Defence Secretary George Robertson's assertion that the UK was 'flying the European flag in the Gulf', an idea that France in particular refused to accept.[14] Most European NATO members eventually backed the US and UK politically or with logistical support, but even those that did were unwilling to take part in any military operations. Germany, Italy and Portugal declared that they would allow US forces to use their air bases to support an attack against Iraq, and Spain authorised the use of a base to support the US airborne refuelling fleet, though not US warplanes.[15] Prodi described his country's support for the US not in terms of a conviction that the threat of force was the right approach, but as Italy 'doing its duty as an ally'. Another Italian official's explanation that it was 'not possible' for Italy 'not to allow' US aircraft to use Italian bases typified a European reaction that suggested reluctance to use force, but unwillingness to defy the US.[16]

France, which was opposed to military force and emphasised the need for a diplomatic solution, was less reluctant to challenge Washington. Paris insisted throughout the crisis that Iraq must comply with Security Council resolutions, and maintained that the use of force was merely 'undesirable', in contrast with Iraq's stand that it was 'unacceptable'.[17] But French officials also repeatedly stressed that a military strike would not accomplish its goals, and they made clear that France would not take part in any military action against Iraq.[18] All indications were that the French public supported its government's stand. One late February poll showed that 75% approved of the government's decision not to participate in a US-led military intervention, compared to 17% who disapproved.

Another poll showed that 55% of the French public believed that France should remain 'totally neutral', with only 10% supporting a French military intervention.[19]

The inspections crisis was resolved – at least temporarily – with a 28 February 1998 agreement between Iraq and UN Secretary-General Kofi Annan that allowed UN inspectors to return. Afterwards, much of France seemed confident that the government's emphasis on diplomacy rather than force had proved correct. Chirac's public-opinion poll ratings rose by 9%; *Le Monde* concluded that it was 'the language of persuasion' that wore Baghdad down; and *Libération* added that 'France proved its capacity to be allied to the Americans while standing up to them during a major crisis'.[20] While acknowledging that the US military mobilisation had also played a critical role in forcing Iraq to back down, Chirac insisted that a lesson of the Iraq crisis was that 'one can obtain the respect of the law, which was our goal, by diplomacy and not only by force'.[21] These conclusions contrasted with the firmly held American and British view that, had it not been for the military build-up and credible threat of force, diplomacy would not have succeeded.

3. The US' Greater Willingness to Act Unilaterally
A third significant difference between the US and most Europeans is Washington's willingness to act unilaterally, in contrast to a preference for multilateral action and decision-making, in particular through the UN. American unilateralism on Iran has been most divisive. In March 1995, citing evidence that Tehran was supporting international terrorism, working to undermine the Middle East peace process and pursuing a nuclear-weapons programme, Clinton forced US oil company Conoco to terminate an exploration deal it had just signed with Iran. Two months later, Clinton imposed a unilateral ban on all US trade with, and investment in, Iran.[22] The fact that the cancelled Conoco deal quickly went to a French firm, Total, exacerbated transatlantic differences on the issue, and led Congress to seek to ensure that it would never happen again. In August 1996, Congress passed the Iran and Libya Sanctions Act (ILSA), sponsored by Republican Senator Alfonse D'Amato. ILSA obliged the President to impose sanctions on any company, whether based in the US or elsewhere, that invested more than $40m in

developing the Iranian or Libyan energy sectors.[23] In contrast to US action on Iraq, where at least the UK and, often, other Europeans accept or at least understand Washington's need for assertive action, EU member-states have unanimously denounced this secondary boycott. Even the most Atlanticist friends of the US criticised the legislation, with EU Trade Commissioner Leon Brittan calling it 'objectionable in principle, contrary to international trade law and damaging to the interests of the European Union'.[24] The EU immediately threatened economic counter-measures if Washington went ahead

confrontation over US sanctions law

with the sanctions, including reviving its suspended challenge at the WTO of another set of extraterritorial US sanctions, the 1995 Helms–Burton Act. The sanctions law was tested in September 1997, when Total announced that, along with Russia's Gazprom and Malaysia's Petronas, it had signed a $2bn agreement to develop Iran's South Pars gas field, setting the stage for a major confrontation.

US unilateralism on Iraq has also been controversial. Many Europeans consider the US linkage of economic sanctions to Saddam's continued rule to be an unacceptable reinterpretation of UN Security Council Resolution 687, which states clearly in paragraph 22 that the embargo on Iraq's exports, essentially oil, should be lifted when the disarmament conditions of the resolution have been fulfilled.[25] France in particular argues that the US position violates both the letter and the spirit of the resolution, and that such unilateral reinterpretations undermine the UN's legitimacy and imperil its global support. For Védrine,

> The lifting of the embargo is subject to precise and logical conditions by paragraph 22 of UN Security Council resolution 687. It will be lifted when these conditions, meaning the dismantlement of the arsenal of weapons of mass destruction, are met.[26]

France stresses, for example in a February 1998 letter from Chirac to Saddam, that, if Iraq cooperates with UN arms inspectors, Paris will support the lifting of sanctions.[27] Even the UK does not officially share the US insistence that Saddam must leave power before sanctions can be lifted, though London seems less optimistic than Paris that Saddam will ever be able to join the international community.[28]

Finally, many Europeans also saw the US decisions to use force in 1993 and 1996, and to prepare for it in 1997–98, as excessively unilateral. The 1993 bombing was denounced by a resolution in the European Parliament for its lack of US consultation with the UN Security Council. Many Europeans criticised the 1996 raids for what they felt was Washington's reluctance to take their opposition into account.[29]

The US stance in the 1997–98 arms-inspection crisis – that it needed no further UN backing for a military strike against Iraq – was most controversial of all. Again, the UK welcomed US willingness to take the action necessary to compel Iraq to grant unfettered access to the UNSCOM inspectors, but other Europeans, especially the French, denounced what they felt was US disregard for the authority of the Security Council.[30] London eventually succeeded in securing a Security Council resolution threatening the 'severest consequences' should Iraq fail to allow the inspectors to do their job. The US insisted that it already had the necessary authority to act and that, in any case, it could justify what it was doing in terms of national interest. Even after the crisis ended, the controversy over the need for UN authorisation continued. The US and UK felt that the solution of the crisis, hard on the heels of the Security Council's threat of severe consequences, implied an 'automatic' military response if Iraq violated the new agreement. French officials, on the other hand, were quick to stress that they still felt that a new Security Council resolution would be needed.[31]

Why do the US and Europe Differ over the Gulf?

Why do Americans and Europeans have different views about Iran and Iraq, and why are their policies dissimilar? At one level, the dispute is the result of a genuine difference in policy analysis about how best to deal with, and eventually change, objectionable regimes. The issue is difficult, and most honest observers would agree that neither American nor European policies towards rogue states can be said, so far, to have 'worked'; Albright admitted as much in March 1998.[32] Debates about the role of military containment in the Gulf continue, and for all the exhaustive academic attempts to determine whether economic sanctions are useful tools of foreign policy, scholars are far from reaching a consensus on the issue.[33]

It would be misleading to conclude, however, that the transatlantic dispute over Iran and Iraq is simply the result of a difference in analysis, and that the positions on the issue could just as easily have been reversed. US and European positions on 'rogue states' in general, and Iran and Iraq in particular, have as much to do with the domestic politics, economic interests, military roles and political cultures of the US and Europe as they do with a dispassionate and disinterested policy dispute.

1. Domestic Politics
Domestic politics have played a crucial role in both US and European approaches towards Iran and Iraq. The American public has still not forgotten the searing experience of the 1979–80 hostage crisis, and Iran's reputation as a supporter of terrorism, its opposition to the Arab–Israeli peace process, reluctance even to meet US officials, and incessant denunciations of the US as the 'Great Satan' inhibit changes in US attitudes. Europeans have also had their problems with Iran (especially the UK, because of a 1989 *fatwa* calling for the death of British author Salman Rushdie), but these are significantly less important than those between Iran and the US. This antipathy towards the Iranian regime can, through the US political process, affect policy in unpredictable ways: ILSA's fate in Congress was uncertain until the bombing of a US military base at Dhahran in Saudi Arabia on 25 June 1996 and the explosion of TWA Flight 800 on 17 July. These incidents made it seem imperative to adopt a tough approach to Iran, even though there was no clear evidence that Tehran was involved in either.[34] ILSA easily passed the Senate on a voice vote, and the House of Representatives by 415 to nil. Taking firm action against Iraq and Libya, whose leaders are seen by many Americans as responsible for acts of international terrorism and aggression, is also popular. Sixty-three per cent of Americans polled in June 1996 supported not only penalising Iran, Libya and Cuba, but also 'punishing foreign companies that do business with Iran, Libya and Cuba by preventing them from selling products in the US'.[35]

The deep American commitment to Israel and the role of the pro-Israeli lobby in Congress also prompt a harder policy line towards Iran and Iraq. AIPAC was closely involved in drafting and lobbying for ILSA, and it was not a coincidence that Clinton's March and May 1995 Executive Orders imposing a near-total economic embargo on Iran were announced at a meeting of major Jewish organisations in Washington.[36] The absence of a similarly strong Jewish lobby in Europe, and Europe's greater economic stake in both Iran and Iraq, mean that its domestic politics often push in the opposite direction.

2. Different Economic Interests
In part because of the US proclivity for imposing economic sanctions on its adversaries, US economic interests in the rogue states of the Middle East, especially since the Iranian revolution, are smaller than those of Europe. This lack of economic interest makes it easier for US leaders to pursue hardline policies. Whereas the US has barely traded with Iran for nearly two decades (even before the 1995 embargo, the US accounted for only some 3% of Iran's imports), EU

Table I *German, French, British and US Trade with Iran, 1990–1997*

(US$m)	1990	1991	1992	1993	1994	1995	1996	1997
Germany								
Imports	2,285	1,427	794	723	752	741	658	1,242
Exports	2,835	4,473	5,612	2,737	1,737	1,812	1,626	1,894
France								
Imports	596	411	609	1,306	908	1,264	1,158	839
Exports	663	985	820	800	907	618	741	806
UK								
Imports	1,512	1,275	1,537	33	185	181	166	54
Exports	766	1,000	1,108	821	484	579	683	713
US								
Imports	294	1,756	2,116	–	1	–	–	–
Exports	140	580	822	678	362	262	–	1

Sources   International Monetary Fund, *Direction of Trade Statistics Yearbook,*
1990–96 (Washington DC: IMF, 1997), p. 256; IMF, *Direction of Trade
Statistics Quarterly*, June 1998, p. 127

states together do more than $11bn in annual business with the country. In 1997, EU exports to Iran were worth $5.5bn, and Iranian exports to the EU $6.1bn.[37] Germany is Iran's main trading partner, and although German exports have fallen from a high of $5.6bn in 1992, Germany still sells $1.9bn of goods and services to Iran each year, accounting for some 35% of EU exports. Italy provides some 19%, France some 15% and the UK 13%.[38] More importantly, Iran's outstanding debt to European countries amounts to over $16bn, of which 20% is owed to Germany, 15% to France and 10% to Italy.[39] This gives Europeans a greater interest than Americans in the health of the Iranian economy, and prompts a strong aversion to sanctions or other measures that might cripple it.

Iraq remains subject to strict Security Council economic sanctions, but some European countries, particularly France and Italy, have important trading relationships with the country that predate the Gulf War. The strong French interest in seeing sanctions lifted is probably related to the fact that Iraq owes France more than $4bn from arms and other deals. Of the approximately $1.3bn in goods that Iraq has been allowed to import with revenues from oil sales under the 'oil-for-food' Resolution 986, France is the leading provider, selling about $200m-worth by 1998.[40] Large oil companies such as Total, Elf Acquitaine and Italy's Agip have, in addition to major investments in Iran, reached preliminary agreements with Iraq on redeveloping the energy sector when sanctions are lifted.

Although the US currently trades with neither Iran nor Iraq, potential US economic interests in these states are not totally absent. In April 1997, a coalition of 630 large US companies formed an organisation called USA Engage to oppose unilateral US trade sanctions abroad, and US-based oil companies such as Mobil, Amoco and Conoco have expressed interest in doing business with Iran.[41] Nonetheless, the greater European economic interaction with Iran and Iraq, as well as with Libya, makes European governments more reluctant than the US to use economic leverage as a foreign-policy tool.

3. Global Security Roles and Perceptions

A third reason why the US takes a harder line on rogue states than Europeans is that Americans see themselves as more responsible for containing threats to international order. As former US National

Security Adviser Anthony Lake put it in 1994, 'As the sole super-power, the United States has a special responsibility for developing a strategy to neutralise ... these backlash states.'[42] If either Iran or Iraq challenges regional or global security, the US, not Europe, must deal with the problem. Iran, Iraq and Libya have all directly challenged Washington's global leadership through propaganda, terrorism and war, and have thereby provoked more hostility from the US than from Europe. US, not European, diplomats and other citizens were held hostage in Iran for over a year during the revolution. US aircraft, servicemen and bases have been targeted by Libyan and Iraqi bombs and missiles. The US took the greatest military risk in leading the international coalition against Saddam in 1991.

The situation in the Gulf is in some ways analogous to the global situation during the Cold War, when the US was the self-appointed and widely accepted leader in the fight against communism, leading to what Europeans often considered excesses in Central America, Asia and even Europe. In

the US, not Europe, is responsible for regional security

the late 1990s, many Americans believe that they remain responsible for coping with challenges to regional or international order, and that Europeans are all too willing to 'free ride' behind them.[43] The perception that the US bears containment's burden while Europe takes advantage of trade was put clearly by Albright in a December 1997 speech to NATO's North Atlantic Council (NAC):

> *I know there is a sense among some Europeans that the US is too inclined to act unilaterally and too quick to pull the sanctions trigger. There is likewise a sense among some Americans that too often the US takes the heat for dealing with difficult issues while others take the contracts – that our willingness to take responsibility for peace and security makes it easier for others to shirk theirs.*[44]

4. US and European Political Cultures

A final explanation for the greater American hostility towards Iran and Iraq is the difference in the political cultures of the US and Europe. Americans, with their idealistic vision of their own place and role in the world, have always been more ready to divide states and causes between 'good' and 'evil'. The strong Wilsonian tradition in foreign policy means that the US has justified its wars in terms of 'making the world safe for democracy' and 'creating a new world order', rather than for explicit reasons of national interest.[45] Europe has a longer and more complicated history, in which most states have at one time or another been either 'good' or 'bad', or both. As a result, Europeans seem more willing to take a moderate view of the behaviour of other countries. US political culture, combined with political structures that make it imperative for leaders to rally public support even for foreign policies, thus seems far more susceptible to the impulse to 'demonise' and to differentiate between 'friends' and 'enemies'. These factors lead Americans to view Iraq and Iran not as merely more problematic than other states, but as adversaries that must be reformed. Europeans are more ready to live with what they believe they cannot change.

Prospects and Strategies for *Rapprochement* in the Gulf

Transatlantic differences over Iraq and Iran thus derive from interests, structures and cultures that are difficult to change. What are the prospects for a convergence of policies, and what strategies might contribute towards it?

Can the Allies Agree on Iraq?

On Iraq, it is not difficult to imagine scenarios that lead to further divergence between the allies. As long as Saddam remains in power, and there appear to be no convincing plans for deposing him, the kinds of crises that have divided the allies in the past could easily recur.

If, for example, Iraq decides to provoke a new crisis with the UN along the lines of those in November 1997, when it expelled US arms inspectors, or in January 1998, when it refused inspectors access to presidential palaces, the same US–European differences on the use of force could emerge, and could worsen if US-led bombing took place. If the US, having reduced significantly its temporary Gulf military build-up of 1997–98, were to undertake another costly deployment in response to Saddam's actions, it would be difficult for Washington not to use force. France would probably distance itself from the bombing and, if civilian casualties started to rise and

Arab anger against the West to grow, other European countries could also be led to do so.

Apparently recognising this possibility – and the lack of European and other allied enthusiasm for using military force to support weapons inspections – the US in mid-1998 appeared to back away from its earlier threats of a near-automatic military response to Iraqi non-cooperation with UNSCOM. When Saddam suspended cooperation with UN arms inspectors in August 1998, Washington did not proceed with a military build-up in the Gulf as it had only nine months previously. Instead, its actions suggested that it would emphasise economic sanctions rather than arms inspections, and would use the threat of force to deter Iraqi aggression or its active pursuit of WMD programmes – but not to support inspections alone.[46] If maintained, this new policy would help to avoid renewed US–European tensions over using force. It was not immediately clear, however, whether the new policy would be sustainable, or whether Saddam would swiftly challenge the international community to the point where Washington felt that military force would have to be threatened again.

Even if Saddam does not provoke a new military crisis with the US, and particularly if he decides to cooperate with the UN, transatlantic disagreement could grow. As time passes and the humanitarian situation in Iraq deteriorates, European pressure for sanctions to be lifted – out of humanitarian concerns, economic interests and fear of the consequences of continued sanctions for relations with the Arab world – will rise. France has already lent its support to Russian calls to ease weapons searches connected to Iraq's nuclear activity, and supports closing the nuclear 'file' while chemical and biological inspections continue.[47] If UNSCOM inspectors certify Iraq as complying with the disarmament provisions of UN Resolution 687, as eventually seems inevitable, a clash between Americans and Europeans (not just France) could ensue. The US might claim that sanctions must be maintained until Iraq satisfied *all* UN resolutions, which would be impossible under Saddam. Many Europeans would call for the letter of Resolution 687 to be respected, which would mean lifting sanctions.

Can such clashes be avoided in a manner consistent with the interests and aims of both the US and Europe? It seems unlikely that the US will soon be ready to lift sanctions on Iraq, particularly in the light of evidence that the regime uses what money it has for Saddam's personal security apparatus and lavish presidential palaces rather than to help the Iraqi people. If Baghdad had access to the more than $115bn in revenues that it has foregone since 1991 by refusing to cooperate with UNSCOM, US officials argue, it would pose an even greater regional threat.[48] The US might find it constructive, however, to clarify its interpretation of Resolution 687, which has always contained at least an element of ambiguity, by making clear that full and total compliance with the resolution's provisions – the elimination of Iraq's nuclear, biological and chemical-weapons capabilities, as well as of its ballistic missiles with a range greater than 150 kilometres – would lead to the lifting of the oil embargo. This would not mean either the end of Iraq's military containment, or of the expressed desire to see Saddam's removal.

the US should clarify its Iraq policy

Even if the embargo on Iraqi exports were lifted, which is all that is called for in Resolution 687, other sanctions, including a full arms embargo, could remain in place, and the US could continue to stress that reintegrating Iraq into the international community would almost certainly depend on its current leader's removal. Such policy clarification would have several merits: it would make it more difficult for Europeans (including Russians) to break with the sanctions regime on the grounds that the US was not obeying the rules; it would help to protect against Arab accusations of double standards where UN resolutions were concerned; and it would give Saddam an incentive to cooperate with UNSCOM, rather than provoke another military confrontation that, in the absence of any inducement not to do so, he has nothing to lose by trying.

Many Americans would be reluctant to take such a course, particularly without a European commitment to maintain Iraq's vigilant containment. This containment policy would have to include a comprehensive and enduring arms embargo, as long as the regime had not changed; strict limits on the trade of dual-use goods; restrictions on investment in Iraq, again until the regime had changed; and, most importantly, a clear threat to use military force against renewed Iraqi aggression or violation of disarmament commitments. Ideally, it would also include European willingness to bear a greater share of the cost of maintaining force-projection capabilities or deploying large-scale military assets in the Gulf. If Europeans want to encourage American willingness to leave 'light at the end of the tunnel' for Iraq, they would help themselves by making these commitments convincingly.

Iran Policy: Sanctions or Dialogue?

The scope for convergence on Iran is wider than on Iraq, though perhaps only because the gaps on Iran have been so great. While differences between the US and Europe persist, two sets of developments since mid-1997 have significantly improved the prospects for a more unified approach. The most important development has been the effect on US policy of the May 1997 election of Mohammed Khatami – an apparently moderate cleric – as Iranian President. Winning by a landslide against the clear preference of the majority of conservative clerics, Khatami immediately began to open up to the US, speaking in interviews and speeches about the need for 'global civil society' and respect for international law, and even praising the 'great American civilisation'.[49] The Clinton administration, having seen its predecessors fail in the search for Iranian 'moderates', remains cautious about what Khatami's election might mean. It has nonetheless concluded that the change is potentially highly significant, and may even call for different policies. While continuing to emphasise those Iranian actions that 'need to be changed', Bruce Riedel, a senior White House Middle East adviser and reportedly a strong supporter of a hard line on Iran, noted in May 1998 that Khatami's election 'obviously marked a milestone in the history of the Islamic Republic' and announced that the US was 'prepared to move further toward engagement'.[50] In June 1998, Clinton himself made clear his belief that Iran under Khatami was 'changing in a positive way', and Albright announced that the US was ready to pursue the 'prospect of a very different relationship' with Iran.[51] Some Congressional attitudes also started to change, in part under belated pressure from the US business community. In April 1998, Congressman Lee Hamilton, who had, like all his House colleagues, voted in favour of ILSA, called the vote a 'mistake', and made an important speech appealing for a new policy of engagement with Iran.[52] USA Engage lobbied for an end to unilateral US sanctions

cautious US opening to Khatami

policy, and the Senate began to consider legislation requiring a cost-benefit analysis of sanctions before they could be approved by Congress.[53]

There have also been important changes on the European side. The Berlin court's 1997 finding that the Iranian government had sponsored terrorism in Germany, along with the desire to avoid a serious clash with the US, has led to a firmer European line towards Tehran. Since mid-1997, while insisting that it refuses to be influenced by the threat of secondary-boycott legislation, the EU has taken measures that go some way towards meeting US demands for a more coercive policy. These include signing anti-terrorism conventions; increasing cooperation on dual-use export controls; announcing an arms embargo; reducing Iranian diplomatic staff in European countries; and foregoing future rescheduling of Iranian debt to EU governments and export agencies.[54] In May 1998, citing the 'significant, enhanced co-operation we have achieved with the European Union' as well as an 'EU commitment to give high priority to proliferation concerns regarding Iran', the US administration agreed not to impose sanctions on Total for its investment in Iran's South Pars gas field.[55] This application of ILSA's 'national interest waiver' (Section 9c), which was part of a broader agreement between the US and the EU to expand trade ties and regulate investment, did not resolve the differences between the US and Europe over investing in Iran, but it went a long way towards keeping them from developing into a damaging trade war.[56]

This relative convergence is promising, but should not be exaggerated. There was no guarantee that Iranian moderates would defeat conservatives, who still held effective power; the EU remained hostile to the very principle of ILSA; and the US administration, if itself divided on the issue, remained under pressure from the Senate, some of whose leading members had urged Clinton to impose sanctions on Total and criticised the subsequent US agreement not to do so.[57] Only a month after the administration made its deal with the EU on ILSA, Congress overwhelmingly passed new legislation, against the wishes of the administration, calling for sanctions to be imposed on companies anywhere in the world supplying Iran with ballistic-missile technology.[58]

Can the gaps be closed further? The search for more unified US–European policies towards Iran should not focus on ideas about how to eliminate the US sanctions legislation that has been at the heart of much of the tension. For better or worse, ILSA will remain in effect until 2001, and will almost certainly not be voted out of existence by Congress before then. Rather, the appropriate aim should be to secure European and American cooperation on common goals, and agreement on a joint package of disincentives and inducements for Iran. The US could continue to consider ILSA as a safeguard against the reversal of either the positive trends in Iran or European cooperation, but it would waive sanctions on European firms (though not necessarily Russian ones) as long as EU states maintained strict controls on dual-use technology, vigilance against terrorism and willingness to respond to Iranian actions that go against Western interests. Taking this route would mean that the US was effectively giving up on that aspect of its policy that seeks to erode Iran's resource base by forcing allies to stop trading with it. Since that approach was in any case not working well, and given the political

what is sanctionable behaviour?

change undoubtedly taking place in Tehran, the moment could be right to pursue gradual engagement. Waiving sanctions on European firms could be a first step that, if reciprocated by Iran in areas of US concern, could be followed by suspending or cancelling the Executive Order banning all US trade with Iran; resolving the issues of frozen Iranian assets and compensation for the US dating back to 1980; beginning official government-to-government talks; and other steps towards normalising ties. Such an approach might not succeed: Iran has its own hardliners who would oppose greater engagement. Nonetheless, it would be more promising than an all-out US effort to punish Iran for its behaviour.

A more united transatlantic approach would also have to include a serious dialogue on what constitutes sanctionable – as opposed to merely objectionable – Iranian behaviour.[59] Is Iranian support for anti-Israeli groups like *Hizbollah* grounds for strict punishment, or rather the pursuit of a national interest that may be condemned, but must also be understood? At what point does Iran's pursuit of nuclear expertise constitute a 'weapons programme' that must be stopped, rather than the sort of precaution that any major state would take in such a troubled region? Is Iran's development of more powerful naval assets in the Gulf an acceptable national-defence measure, or a threat to Western interests that must at all costs be constrained? Transatlantic dialogue on these difficult issues would not easily produce a common set of guidelines, but a serious attempt to narrow the differences on key points would be useful. The US has a right to ask its European allies if there are *any* Iranian actions that would necessitate sanctions – unambiguous evidence of a nuclear-weapons programme or state-sponsored terrorism against American or European citizens or forces, for example. Europe should have the opportunity to persuade the US that some Iranian policies, such as repressing dissident groups or spending on conventional weapons, should not be grounds for sanctions. Progress towards identifying the actions that fall under each category would improve the prospects for unified and effective transatlantic policies.

Finally, it will be necessary for the US to make clear that containment policy in the Gulf is not designed to last forever, but to bring about the changes necessary for it to end. Just as Reagan was prepared to adapt to change in the Soviet Union when it became meaningful under Mikhail Gorbachev, so the US should emphasise that it remains ready to end the 'cold war' with Iran as soon as Tehran is ready. It is unclear whether Khatami is an 'Iranian Gorbachev', but, if he is, the US should stress that it is as ready to change its policies now as it was then.

Coordinating Western Policy

This paper argues that the differences between Europe and the US on the Middle East are detrimental to common interests because they limit the effectiveness of transatlantic policies towards the region, undermine the cohesion of the Atlantic Alliance and threaten transatlantic commercial relations. Such differences are at times impossible to avoid because they result from historical, cultural, geographic, economic and domestic political factors that are difficult to change. But it should also be clear that transatlantic friction on the Middle East is not inevitable. Since their broad interests and values in the region are similar, the US and Europe have agreed on both the Gulf and the peace process before, and there is no inherent reason why they cannot do so again. Transatlantic accord has largely depended upon developments within the region. When Arabs and Israelis are moving towards peace and there is a clear threat to Western interests from the Gulf, Americans and Europeans tend to rally together and advocate similar policies. When the peace process breaks down and Gulf issues become more ambiguous, as has been the case since the mid-1990s, transatlantic disagreements grow.

A case could be made that US–Europe differences over the Middle East are not a vice but a virtue, and that the best response is not to fight against divergent approaches, but to take advantage of the benefits each side has to offer. The Europeans can maintain useful contacts and pursue dialogue with Palestinians, the Iranian government and Saddam, while the US stands as Israel's protector and wields the threat of military force and economic pressure. This type of division of labour is similar to that of certain periods of the Cold War, when Europeans pursued *détente* with the Soviet Union, while Americans emphasised economic isolation and deterrence. Strategies such as these arguably proved effective in the February 1998 stand-off with Iraq, when the US and UK made military threats and France and Russia advanced diplomatic initiatives. As French Foreign Minister Védrine rightly put it, 'if there had been only threats without acceptable diplomatic proposals, it would not have succeeded, and if there had been only proposals without threats it would not have succeeded'.[1]

Making the most of a bad situation, however, is neither the same nor as good as having a common strategy that incorporates both inducements and restraints. Any reasonable strategy of containment should include ways to improve relations, as well as means of dialogue when there is something to discuss. Any reasonable strategy of engagement should not be without the means to deter unacceptable behaviour. The negative consequences of the division-of-labour approach, moreover, should not be ignored. When the US and Europe are on opposite sides of Middle East issues, the parties to these conflicts can be led to believe that they do not have to compromise because they have an outside advocate. This can prolong, rather than help to resolve, diplomatic stalemates. Given the collective strength of the world's two largest economies and its most advanced military powers, a common transatlantic approach is more likely to be effective.

Even more mistaken is the idea that transatlantic differences can be helpful on the question of deterrence – the threat of using military force to dissuade Iran or Iraq from some specified action. French warnings that the use of force against Iraq in early 1998 would not succeed may or may not have been correct, but they were inconsistent with the attempt by the US and UK to make credible their threat of a military strike. A unified Alliance position that threatens force, but is also willing to pursue diplomacy, is better than individual allies following different courses. When a strategy comprising hard and soft approaches is necessary, it is usually easier to find candidates to provide the soft line than it is to find those willing to bear the burdens and risks of the harder approach.

What could happen if the allies fail to agree on the Middle East? While the negative consequences of disagreement should not be exaggerated – the Alliance remains strong enough to survive even sharp disagreements – some grave scenarios can be imagined. If the Middle East peace process continues to deteriorate, for example, so will transatlantic relations over the issue. If the US acquiesces too readily to Israeli policies that Europeans find unacceptable, some Europeans, even those traditionally reluctant to do so, might begin to advocate a more independent approach, leading to a diplomatic clash with the US. Europeans primarily blame the Netanyahu government for the lack of progress in the peace process, and European support for Palestinians should violence resume in the West Bank could easily lead to mutual recriminations across the Atlantic. More specifically, transatlantic disagreement could be in store in May 1999, when Yasser Arafat's PA has vowed unilaterally to declare a Palestinian state if the final-status talks foreseen in the Oslo agreement are not complete.

The US has announced that it opposes such a declaration, and would 'most likely' not recognise a unilaterally declared state. Europeans would almost certainly do so (a fact that itself may make the declaration more likely).[2] It is one thing for the allies to have differing views on how to approach the Middle East peace process. It is quite another to imagine a situation in which Europe recognised a new state, presumably with all the rights of self-defence implied by statehood and the UN membership that could follow, that the US did not recognise. Unilaterally declaring a Palestinian state could lead Israel to annex territory in the West Bank, possibly leading to open conflict with armed Palestinians backed by other states in the Middle East and supported by Europeans. The consequences for transatlantic relations, let alone for the Middle East, should not be underestimated. A major US–Europe clash in the Middle East in May 1999 would make a mockery of the statements of transatlantic unity that will doubtless be issued at the NATO summit in Washington just a month before.

Avoiding such a scenario calls for closer coordination between the US and its European allies on a strategy to manage a possible declaration of Palestinian statehood. In a common approach, neither Americans nor Europeans would declare in advance whether they would recognise a Palestinian state, but would use the possibility of doing so – or of withholding recognition – as leverage against the regional parties. The allies would make it clear to the PA that they would not recognise a Palestinian state unless the Authority demonstrated its determination to fight terrorism against Israel, excised definitively from the PLO Charter any question about Israel's right to exist, showed itself willing to live in peace with its neighbours within recognised borders and accepted an arms-control regime. At the same time, the US and Europe would make it equally clear to Israel that they would find it difficult *not* to recognise a Palestinian state if Israel remained reluctant to implement the Oslo accords in good faith. Given the domestic political and other constraints on each side of the Atlantic, maintaining a common position on this issue would be difficult, but the potential gains of such an approach make it worthwhile. This type of coordinated strategy is also a good example of the appropriate US and European roles in the peace process that are described in this paper. Whatever the merits of the issue, a European initiative to recognise a Palestinian state without US support is likely to lead to transatlantic recriminations, and is unlikely to further the cause of stability in the region. A common US–European approach maximises the leverage of both, and offers the greatest chance of success.

the costs of transatlantic disagreement are clear

On Iraq, the potential costs of transatlantic disagreement are also clear. It is likely that one of the reasons why Saddam provoked the 1997–98 inspections crisis was that he felt the international community was divided and could be further split. There is no doubt that Iraq could try such a tactic again. The crisis also demonstrated the division between Americans and some Europeans over using force against Iraq. If Iraqi actions lead the US to implement the bombing campaign that it threatened in early 1998, these transatlantic splits could be far more damaging. American resentment would be high if US pilots and soldiers were killed in large numbers during a conflict with Iraq and Europeans were not standing by the US in defence of what Americans perceive to be shared transatlantic vital interests. Europeans might remember their own resentment of the US during the Yugoslav wars of the early 1990s, when Europeans were dying in defence of perceived common interests and the US was seen to be meddling from the outside, but not engaged on the ground.

Without agreement on a common policy, Iraq could also provoke divisions in the Alliance if it pursues a strategy of apparent cooperation, rather than confrontation. If Europeans conclude that Iraq has satisfied its disarmament obligations under UN Security Council Resolution 687, they might invoke a legal right to begin trading with Iraq even while the US insists that sanctions must be maintained. Europeans might feel that the US would be unable to sustain this position if the rest of the Security Council agreed that its conditions had been satisfied, but the potential for Congress to force the administration to stand firm should not be underestimated. This is all the more true as such a crisis might easily become caught up in the political campaign for the presidential and Congressional elections in 2000, much as US Iran policy was entangled with the 1996 elections. European commerce with an Iraq still seen by the US as a threat to its vital interests would be detrimental to transatlantic cooperation.

The best way to avoid such scenarios is for Europeans to accept the continued need for economic sanctions and military containment – along with efforts to overthrow the regime if possible – and for Americans to offer incentives to prompt Iraq to abide by its obligations under UN Security Council resolutions. Until Baghdad complies fully with UN disarmament provisions, economic sanctions, military containment and efforts to topple Saddam are necessary, since Iraq with WMD would pose a threat to the region and the world. Failure to insist on these provisions would not only take great risks with regional security, but would also send a negative message about the international community's resolve. At the same time, offering incentives to prompt Iraqi compliance is necessary. Doing so would protect the US and Europe from Arab accusations of double standards; make it easier to keep the anti-Iraq coalition together; and give Baghdad a reason to do as the West wishes. No policy option to deal with Saddam is ideal, but combining strict containment with a 'light at the end of the tunnel' offers the best hope not only of transatlantic unity on the issue, but also, more importantly, of achieving common aims.

Finally, the potentially damaging consequences of the lack of an agreed strategy on Iran have been amply demonstrated. Fortunately, the reform process in Tehran, and growing American willingness to pursue cautious engagement, increases the possibility that the deep disagreements of 1995–98 will prove a passing phase. It is, however, too early to conclude that the potential for fresh transatlantic disagreement has disappeared, and a setback to the reform process in Iran could easily provoke renewed dispute over how to respond. The US Congress has not renounced its preference for denying resources and for coercion to achieve its goals. Any one of several developments – evidence of an accelerated Iranian WMD programme, Iran's support for violence against Israel or cases of Iranian-sponsored terrorism abroad, for example – could result in a new US campaign, possibly including reviving extraterritorial legislation against Europe. A modernising, reformist evolution of Iranian politics would probably produce transatlantic cooperation on engagement, but a setback to that process could provoke the sort of transatlantic disagreement that was so damaging in 1995–98.

Setting common standards for normalising ties with the Iranian regime would be most likely to avoid such a scenario. These standards, though difficult to achieve, would be better than the current situation, in which European engagement with Tehran has been virtually unconditional, while the US has not engaged with Iran at all. For a common strategy to become possible, the US would first have to refrain from efforts to compel Europe to cooperate by using extraterritorial sanctions, the costs of which have outweighed the benefits. Washington would also have to agree that not *all* objectionable Iranian policies – repressing dissidents, maintaining nuclear expertise or acquiring conventional weapons, for example – are grounds for refusing dialogue or trade. This will be particularly the case if the Khatami regime continues to reach out to the West, and Iranian society becomes more pluralistic. Europeans, on the other hand, would have to agree that *some* Iranian policies – an active nuclear-weapons programme, state support for terrorism, particularly against Western targets, and support for violence designed to destroy the Middle East peace process – *should* trigger meaningful diplomatic or economic sanctions. Europeans and Americans may never agree on precisely where these lines should be drawn, but their interests should be sufficiently similar to achieve a common framework that would present Iran with a clearer indication of the costs and benefits of its actions.

Where should transatlantic cooperation on the Middle East take place? The key bilateral relationships will continue to play the most important role in coordinating transatlantic policies. Beyond them, there is no shortage of institutional mechanisms that can serve as useful forums for elaborating common approaches. NATO is the appropriate forum for US–European military cooperation, and the organisation's development of a counter-proliferation policy since 1994 is a useful contribution to a common strategy for the Middle East. NATO is also the right place to develop joint US–European power-projection capabilities for the Middle East, particularly the Gulf. New military command structures specifically designed for this purpose are currently too controversial, and probably unnecessary. Nonetheless, the Alliance should make clear, in its new Strategic Concept and at the April 1999 Washington summit, that it considers peace and stability in the Middle East an appropriate issue for its attention and a legitimate area of operation. Some European governments are understandably reluctant to turn NATO into a platform for global US military actions, and are concerned about offending Arab states around the Mediterranean by giving NATO an explicit 'out-of-area' role. Nonetheless, making NATO more relevant to the post-Cold War security issues that Americans find most important would help to maintain the support of the US public and Congress for the US–European alliance more generally. The European NATO allies may not be ready to commit in advance to a power-projection initiative for the Middle East but, given the region's importance and the limited resources available for defence, it would be a mistake not to take advantage of NATO's common infrastructure, inter-operable armed forces and long history of military cooperation.

A case could be made that NATO's role in coordinating Western policy towards the Middle East should be further upgraded, and that the NAC should become the key forum for transatlantic discussions of the issue. Under this scenario, NATO's Secretary-General would become a kind of foreign-policy 'High Representa-tive' for the Atlantic Alliance, and would coordinate discussions not just of security policy, but of foreign policy more broadly, including for the Middle East. The US Permanent Representative to NATO would be given a greater role in framing US foreign policy, and would possibly receive Cabinet status like the US Ambassador to the UN. The EU's CFSP, as it developed, would be brought into the NATO process and represented at the NAC. Ideas such as these, although intriguing and consistent with the logic of developing common US and European approaches, are probably premature. The CFSP is not sufficiently developed to represent the EU at NATO; the EU's non-NATO members with an interest in the Middle East would be excluded; and, in any case, Washington is not ready to devolve significant Middle East policymaking responsibility to Brussels. It is right that NATO should consider and debate the non-military aspects of security, but it is probably unrealistic to expect the organisation to play a much more ambitious political and economic role in the near future.

A more realistic goal might be to expand the foreign-policy role of the still-embryonic New Transatlantic Agenda (NTA), an initiative begun with the 1990 US–EU 'Transatlantic Declaration' and strengthened at the December 1995 EU–US Madrid summit.[3] The main merit of the under-used NTA is that it has institutionalised twice-yearly meetings between the US President and his most important EU counterparts, the President of the Commission, the holder of the rotating EU presidency, and the EU Trade Commissioner. This offers a regular forum for dialogue and action among the key transatlantic players. Despite its ambitious aims – to promote peace and stability; respond to global challenges; develop world trade; and foster transatlantic links – the NTA has so far not emerged as the key forum that it has the potential to become. Making it a forum for dealing with the issue of transatlantic cooperation on the Middle East could thus help not only to resolve differences over the region, but also to give substance to the fledgling institution. The 18 May 1998 summit in London, at which the US and EU announced their compromise on secondary-boycott legislation and a common framework for investment in sensitive countries, was a clear example of how the NTA can be put to good use. Without the deadline of the summit and the pressure to reach an agreement so that other business could proceed, the issue might have languished longer than it did.

Beyond specifically US–European institutions, the Group of Eight (G-8) industrial nations is another appropriate forum for transatlantic dialogue and action on Middle East issues. It has the merit of including not only the most important North Atlantic and European allies and Japan, but also Russia, a key actor where proliferation, arms control, and Security Council-related issues arise. Just as unilateral American initiatives on the Middle East are unlikely to succeed if they are not backed by the European allies, common transatlantic policies can be undermined if not supported by Russia. The G-8 should link the financial cooperation and international respect so highly valued by Russia to Moscow's cooperation in non-proliferation and combating terrorism in the Middle East.

Finally, and perhaps most importantly, Europeans need to find a way to open a dialogue with key members of the US Congress – the source of much of the transatlantic friction over the Middle East. There should be no illusions that Congress will pay more attention to the arguments of the Europeans than to the perceived interests of its constituents. There is nonetheless scope for greater European dialogue and lobbying, which could at least provide an opportunity to prevent some of the more damaging transatlantic splits.

Transatlantic agreement on contentious issues in the Middle East can never be guaranteed. Countries' specific national interests must sometimes take priority over the general goal of good relations between Atlantic partners. Nonetheless, these perceived interests must be continually weighed against the costs of a divided Western approach. The benefits of compromise in the name of common policies will sometimes be worth the sacrifice. Common strategies – whether towards the Middle East peace process, Iraq or Iran – maximise Western leverage and have a far greater chance of success than the divided approach of the late 1990s.

notes

The author benefited from comments on earlier drafts of this paper by a number of European and American experts, and would in particular like to thank, in addition to colleagues at the IISS, Gilles Andreani, Christoph Bertram, Richard Gozney, Richard Haass, Mark Heller, Rosemary Hollis, Ibrahim Karawan, Geoffrey Kemp, Ken Pollack, John Roper, Gideon Rose, Gary Sick and Paul Taylor. Marine Gergorin, Marta Golonka and Helga Haack provided valuable research assistance. The American Institute for Contemporary German Studies, Washington DC, generously hosted a workshop at which a draft of this paper was presented.

Introduction

[1] For the case that European failure to support US global strategy will undermine NATO, see Ronald D. Asmus, Robert Blackwill and F. Stephen Larrabee, 'Can NATO Survive?', *Washington Quarterly*, vol. 19, no. 2, Spring 1996, pp. 79–101; and David C. Gompert and F. Stephen Larrabee, *America and Europe: A Partnership for a New Era* (Cambridge: Cambridge University Press, 1997). Also see Senator John Warner's caution to Europeans during the 1998 crisis with Iraq: 'Make no mistake, there is a direct relationship between decisions taken on Iraq in the next few weeks and US support for NATO.' Martin Walker, 'East–West "Partners" Feel Strain', *The Guardian*, 10 February 1998, p. 11.

[2] See, for example, Robert D. Blackwill and Michael Stürmer (eds), *Allies Divided: Transatlantic Policies for the Greater Middle East* (Cambridge, MA: Massachusetts Institute of Technology (MIT) Press, 1997).

[3] Some analysts consider the 'Greater Middle East' to stretch from Morocco in the west to India in the east, and from Kazakstan in the north to Somalia in the south. Others distinguish 'the Middle

East' from 'North Africa' and 'the Gulf', and include only Israel, Lebanon, Syria and Egypt. For the first and wider definition (as well as a discussion of alternatives), see Geoffrey Kemp and Robert E. Harkavy, *Strategic Geography and the Changing Middle East* (Washington DC: Carnegie Endowment for International Peace, 1997), pp. 13–14. For the narrower definition, see *The Military Balance 1996/97* (Oxford: Oxford University Press for the IISS, 1997), pp. 120–21.

⁴ For the sake of simplicity and clarity, this paper uses the shorthand 'the Middle East' when referring to the region as a whole, and, more specifically, 'the Arab–Israeli dispute', 'the Middle East peace process' or 'the Gulf' when referring to only one of its two sub-regions.

Chapter 1

¹ Sadat later admitted privately that 'the United States actually holds only 60 percent of the cards'. Nonetheless, as Daniel Yergin has noted, this 'was certainly more than adequate reason to lean toward the United States'. See Yergin, *The Prize: The Epic Quest for Oil, Money, and Power* (New York: Simon & Schuster, 1991), p. 627.

² On the early balance between US 'oil interests' and 'Israel interests', see Michael C. Hudson, 'To Play the Hegemon: Fifty Years of US Policy Toward the Middle East', *Middle East Journal*, vol. 50, no. 3, Summer 1996, pp. 332–35.

³ See *Europa-Archiv*, no. 2, 1974, p. D30.

⁴ See 'Declaration of the European Council on the Euro–Arab Dialogue and the Situation in the Middle East', European Council, Venice, 12–13 June 1980. Excerpts from the text can be found in Walter Laqueur and Barry Rubin (eds), *The Israel–Arab Reader: A Documentary History of the Middle East Conflict* (New York: Penguin, 1995), pp. 414–15.

⁵ See David Makovsky, *Making Peace with the PLO: The Rabin Government's Road to the Oslo Accord* (Boulder, CO: Westview Press, 1996).

⁶ See European Union, *Bulletin EU 4–1996*, 22 April 1996, available at www.europa.eu.int; 'Le Massacre de Cana', *Le Monde*, 20 April 1996, p. 2; 'Rencontres Décisives à Damas pour le Cessez-le-Feu au Liban', *ibid.*, 22 April 1996, p. 2; and Françoise Chipaux, 'La Crise Libanaise', *ibid.*, 23 April 1996, p. 2.

⁷ See 'EU Declaration on the Middle East Peace Process', *European Union Press Release No. 56/96*, 1 October 1996.

⁸ French Foreign Minister Hervé de Charette admitted that special envoy Moratinos' role would not be to 'get a seat at a table where we are not wanted', but concluded that Europe's co-sponsorship of the peace process would 'eventually come about'. See Philippe Lemaître, 'Un Emissaire au Mandat Encore Imprécis pour le Proche-Orient', *Le Monde*, 30 October 1996, p. 4.

⁹ See Samuel Lewis, paper presented to the Washington Institute for Near East Policy's 1996 Policy Conference 'Toward 2000: Middle East Challenges for the Next Administration', Washington DC, 18–20 October 1996, p. 39.

¹⁰ See the EU's charge in the 'Luxembourg Declaration' that the clashes between Israeli troops and Palestinian Authority (PA) security

forces in September 1996 'were precipitated by frustration and exasperation at the absence of any real progress in the Peace Process'. 'EU Declaration on the Middle East Peace Process', p. 1.

[11] Interview with French Foreign Ministry official, September 1997.

[12] As Prime Minister in 1974–76 – during the first oil crisis – Chirac had been deeply involved in the Middle East, and had particularly close ties to Saddam Hussein's Iraq. On the impetus Chirac gave to French Middle East policy, see David Makovsky, 'Behind Chirac's Foreign Policy Activism', *Jerusalem Post*, 25 October 1996, p. 9; and Barry James, 'Strong Ties to Arab Nations Are Key to French Foreign Policy, Chirac Says', *International Herald Tribune*, 9 April 1996, p. 5.

[13] Chirac quoted in Mouna Naïm, 'Paris Veut Faire Avaliser Son Rôle au Proche-Orient', *Le Monde*, 10 July 1996, p. 5.

[14] Remarks by EU official Peter Carter at Emory University, Atlanta, GA, 7 October 1996 quoted in Kenneth W. Stein, 'Will Europe and America Ever Agree?', *Middle East Quarterly*, vol. 14, no. 1, March 1997, p. 42.

Chapter 2

[1] On shared interests between the US and Europe, see Zalmay Khalilzad, 'Challenges in the Greater Middle East', in Gompert and Larrabee (eds), *America and Europe*, pp. 194–201. Also see Blackwill and Stürmer (eds), *Allies Divided*.

[2] The 'Luxembourg Declaration' reaffirmed the EU position that 'East Jerusalem is subject to the principles set out in UN Security Council Resolution 242, notably the inadmissibility of the acquisition of territory by force and is therefore not under Israeli sovereignty'. Europeans strongly oppose US Congressional legislation to move the US Embassy from Tel Aviv to Jerusalem (which would make the US one of only a small number of countries to have done so). Moving the embassy would *de facto* mean siding with Israel on the debate over Jerusalem's future, breaking with the US' declared policy of leaving the final status of the city open to negotiated agreement.

[3] In February 1997, the EU signed an Association Agreement, along the lines of those with Tunisia, Morocco and Israel, with the PA. See Jean Quatremer, 'Les Quinze Offrent une Bouffée d'Air à Arafat', *Libération*, 25 February 1997.

[4] See Satloff, 'America, Europe and the Middle East', p. 13. For a similar expression of the US role in the peace process by a senior US negotiator, see Deputy Special Middle East Coordinator Aaron David Miller, 'The US Role in the Peace Process: A Perspective', *PolicyWatch*, no. 153, Washington Institute for Near East Policy, 17 February 1998.

[5] The Commission on US–Israel Relations included nearly all the key foreign-policy players in Clinton's forthcoming administration: Madeleine Albright, Les Aspin, Samuel Berger, Stuart Eizenstat, Leon Fuerth, Martin Indyk, Anthony Lake, Samuel Lewis, Clark Murdock and Walter Slocombe. See *Enduring Partnership: Report of the Commission on US–Israel Relations* (Washington DC: Washington Institute for Near East Policy, 1993).

[6] See Stephen P. Cohen's contribution to *US Middle East*

Policy and the Peace Process: Report of an Independent Task Force Sponsored by the Council on Foreign Relations (New York: Council on Foreign Relations, 1997). Cohen argued that 'American activism, American peace leadership is *not* to declare the substance of potential agreement' (p. 32).

[7] Israeli Prime Minister Binyamin Netanyahu described his vision of the US negotiating role in terms similar to those used by US officials. The US should play a role as a 'facilitator and sometimes a mediator, but certainly not [one] in which it assumes or takes over the responsibility of trying to establish a position … the parties themselves must come to an agreement from and within themselves. That is the only kind of an agreement that sticks'. See excerpts from a speech delivered by Netanyahu to the Washington Institute for Near East Policy, Washington DC, 14 May 1998, published in 'Special Policy Forum Report: Israeli Prime Minister Benjamin Netanyahu', *PeaceWatch*, no. 165, Washington Institute for Near East Policy, 18 May 1998.

[8] The Commission's logic was apparently that Israel saw EU aid to the Palestinians as in its interests, and would seek to avoid the cut-off. See 'The Role of the European Union in the Middle East Peace Process and Its Future Assistance', *Executive Summary of the Communication to the Council of Ministers and the European Parliament*, European Commission, 16 January 1998; and Martin Walker, 'EU Seeks Bigger Role in Middle East Peace', *The Guardian*, 17 January 1998, p. 18.

[9] US Ambassador to the UN Bill Richardson quoted in 'A Principled Veto', *Jerusalem Post*, 9 March 1997,

p. 6; and United Nations, 'Security Council Again Fails to Adopt Resolution on Israeli Settlement', *Press Release SC/6345*, 21 March 1997. On the US attempt to block the UN resolution criticising Israel for the *Grapes of Wrath* operation in 1996, see 'Washington Empêche le Conseil de Sécurité de Voter un Texte sur le Liban', *Le Monde*, 17 April 1996, p. 2.

[10] Clinton quoted in 'Remarks by the President and Prime Minister Netanyahu in Photo Opportunity with King Hussein of Jordan, Prime Minister Netanyahu and PLO Chairman Arafat', The White House, Office of the Press Secretary, 1 October 1996. A month earlier, Clinton had dismissed speculation that the US was going to take a tougher stance towards Israel by saying that 'the US doesn't enter into the equation as someone who pressures'. See Sarah Honig and Hillel Kuttler, 'Albright Expected to be Tough on Israel', *Jerusalem Post*, 9 September 1997, p. 1.

[11] When asked after a meeting with Netanyahu in January 1998 whether the US had 'pressured' Israel to agree to a redeployment, Clinton replied: 'I wouldn't use that word ['pressure']. Israel has to make its own decisions about security.' See John F. Harris, 'An Initial Meeting of Clinton and Netanyahu Yields Little Progress', *International Herald Tribune*, 21 January 1998, p. 1. On the US threat to 're-examine' its approach to Israel, see Barton Gellman, 'Clinton Sets a Course of Confrontation', *ibid.*, 11 May 1998, p. 1.

[12] Clinton quoted in Brian Knowlton, 'Mrs Clinton Starts Storm By Backing "Palestine"', *ibid.*, 8 May 1998, p. 1.

[13] See unnamed European official quoted in Barton Gelman, 'US Signals Retreat from Pressure on Israel', *Washington Post*, 23 July 1998, pp. A1, A25. The official added that 'the received wisdom is that the Israelis do nothing under pressure, to which I'd say they certainly do nothing *not* under pressure'.

[14] Egypt receives $815 million in economic aid and $1.3 billion in military aid annually; Israel receives $1.2bn and $1.8bn respectively. See *Congressional Presentation, Summary Tables Fiscal Year 1998* (Washington DC: US Agency for International Development, 1998), pp. 13, 19, 25.

[15] All but $80m of Israel's $1.2bn of 'economic' aid is used to repay military debts, meaning that 97% of the total US aid package to Israel is related to security. In May 1998, Israel and the US agreed to reduce the annual economic-assistance programme by $120m each year beginning in 1999, in exchange for an increase in US military aid of $60m a year. Within ten years, according to this arrangement, Israel would no longer receive economic aid from the US, but its annual military-aid package would have risen by $600m. See Barbara Opall-Rome, 'Israel, US, Reach Aid Compromise', *Defense News*, 11–17 May 1998, p. 24; and Serge Schmemann, 'Israeli's Quest in Washington: Less Aid', *International Herald Tribune*, 28 January 1998, p. 7.

[16] See European Commission, 'The Role of the European Union'; and Walker, 'EU Seeks Bigger Role'.

[17] See Stephen Erlanger, 'Pro-Israel Lobby in US Wields Discreet Power', *International Herald Tribune*, 27 April 1998, p. 2; and J. J. Goldberg, *Jewish Power: Inside the American Jewish Establishment* (Reading, MA: Addison-Wesley, 1998), pp. 15, 197–226.

[18] See Lawrence Wright, 'Letter from Jerusalem', *The New Yorker*, 20 July 1998.

[19] See *International Petroleum Statistics Report* (Washington DC: US Department of Energy, 1996).

[20] See *British Petroleum Statistical Review of World Energy 1996* (London: British Petroleum Company, 1996), pp. 18, 28; and *Persian Gulf Oil Export Fact Sheet* (Washington DC: United States Energy Information Administration, 1997). According to some projections, Europe will in 2010 import up to eight million barrels of oil per day from the Gulf alone, compared with less than 4.5m by the US. See Kemp and Harkavy, *Strategic Geography*, p. 118.

[21] See Zalmay M. Khalilzad, David A. Shlapak and Daniel L. Byman, *The Implications of the Possible End of the Arab–Israeli Conflict for Gulf Security* (Santa Monica, CA: RAND, 1997), pp. 35–51.

[22] See Michael R. Gordon and General Bernard E. Trainor, *The Generals' War* (Boston, MA: Little, Brown, 1995), pp. 291–99.

[23] For a general discussion of the issue of US–Israeli strategic relations, see Shai Feldman, *The Future of US–Israel Strategic Cooperation* (Washington DC: Washington Institute for Near East Policy, 1996).

[24] See, for example, Helmut Hubel, 'Germany and the Middle East Conflict', in Shahram Chubin (ed.), *Germany and the Middle East: Patterns and Prospects* (London: Pinter, 1992), pp. 41–54; and Josef Joffe, 'Reflections on German Policy in the Middle East', in *ibid.*, pp. 195–209.

[25] See Lemaître, 'Un Emissaire au Mandat Encore Imprécis pour le Proche-Orient'; and Stein, 'Will Europe and America Ever Agree?', p. 42.

[26] See 'Seeking Role, Chirac Ruffles Israeli Feathers', *International Herald Tribune*, 21 October 1997; and 'Chirac in Damascus: Peace Process in Danger, EU Must Intervene', *Reuters*, 20 October 1996.

[27] France's more far-reaching ideas, such as creating a 'Mr CFSP' with authority to coordinate and express European foreign policy, were diluted at the EU Intergovernmental Conference (IGC) in Amsterdam in June 1997. See Philip H. Gordon, 'The Limits to Europe's Common Foreign and Security Policy', in Andrew Moravcsik (ed.), *Centralization or Fragmentation? Europe Before the Challenges of Deepening, Diversity, and Democracy* (Washington DC: Brookings Institution/Council on Foreign Relations, 1998).

[28] Italian Foreign Minister Susanna Agnelli argued in 1996 that France should have deferred to the EU. See 'Italy Warns France on Mideast Missions', *International Herald Tribune*, 11 May 1996, p. 2.

[29] During his Middle East visit, Chirac said that only a Palestinian state would provide Israel with the sort of partner that it needed for security. See David Rudge, 'Chirac: Only a Palestinian State Will Bring Security to Israel', *Jerusalem Post*, 22 October 1996, p. 1.

[30] Klaus Kinkel interviewed on Syrian Television, 6 July 1995, quoted in Satloff, 'America, Europe, and the Middle East', p. 31. Also see Lemaître, 'Un Emissaire au Mandat Encore Imprécis pour le Proche-Orient'.

[31] See Malcolm Rifkind, 'Blueprint for a Region at Peace', *The Times*, 5 November 1996, p. 20. For Dick Spring's comments, see Judy Dempsey and Alexandra Capelle, 'Israel: Chirac Calls for European Involvement in Peace Plans', *Financial Times*, 24 October 1996, p. 3.

[32] See European Commission, 'The Role of the European Union', p. 4; and Barry James, 'Europe Seeks Bigger Role in Mideast Peace Process', *International Herald Tribune*, 17–18 January 1998.

[33] See Eberhard Rhein, 'Europe and the Greater Middle East', in Blackwill and Stürmer (eds), *Allies Divided*, p. 59.

[34] On the Troika in the Gulf, see Carlos Zaldivar and Andrés Ortega, 'The Gulf Crisis and European Cooperation on Security Issues: Spanish Reactions and the European Framework', in Nicole Gnesotto and John Roper (eds), *Western Europe and the Gulf* (Paris: Institute for Security Studies of the Western European Union, 1992), p. 131. On the general problem with the Troika and EU foreign-policy representation, see Gordon, 'The Limits of Europe's Common Foreign and Security Policy'.

[35] See Rosemary Hollis, 'Europe and the Middle East: Power by Stealth?', *International Affairs*, vol. 73, no. 1, January 1997, pp. 15–29.

[36] See Haass, 'The United States, Europe, and the Middle East Peace Process', pp. 61–62.

[37] See Satloff, 'America, Europe, and the Middle East', p. 36.

[38] See Zuckerman and Pollack's contribution to *US Middle East Policy*, p. 28.

[39] *US Middle East Policy* (pp. 20–21) calls for 'far greater co-ordination' with the Europeans, and adds that this more collaborative role should be 'under American leadership'.

Also see Khalilzad, 'Challenges in the Greater Middle East', pp. 191–217.

[40] See interview with Israeli Defence Minister Yitzhak Mordechai, 'Paris Doit "Mener la Médiation" Entre Israël et le Liban', *Le Figaro*, 19 March 1998; and Leslie Susser, 'New Approach to a Deal on Lebanon', *Jerusalem Report*, 19 February 1998.

[41] See Mouna Naïm, 'Un Projet de Conférence pour la Paix qui Embarrasse Israël', *Le Monde*, 16 July 1998, p. 2; and Mouna Naïm, 'L'Egypte et la France Cherchent les Moyens de Sauver le Processus de Paix', *ibid.*, 29 July 1998, p. 2.

[42] Netanyahu has spoken of 'restrained self-determination' and made analogies with entities like Puerto Rico and Andorra. See 'Altered States', *Jerusalem Post*, 11 November 1996, p. 6. For a discussion of Israeli attitudes towards a Palestinian state, see Mark A. Heller, 'Towards a Palestinian State', *Survival*, vol. 39, no. 2, Summer 1997, pp. 5–22.

[43] See Efraim Inbar and Shmuel Sandler, 'The Risks of Palestinian Statehood', *ibid.*, p. 23.

[44] Richard Haass argues that the Palestinians were 'prepared to look the other way during Labor's tenure only because they had confidence in its commitment to peace'. See Haass, 'The Middle East: No More Treaties', *Foreign Affairs*, vol. 75, no. 5, September–October 1996, p. 60.

[45] See Matthew Dorf, 'Jews Critical of Current Israeli Policies', *Washington Jewish Week*, 26 February 1998; Jonathan Broder, 'Netanyahu and American Jews', *World Policy Journal*, vol. 15, no. 1, Spring 1998, pp. 89–98; and J. J. Goldberg, 'The Fighting Family', *Jerusalem Report*, 11 December 1997,

pp. 34–35. For a good discussion of American Jewish attitudes towards Israel in general, see Goldberg, *Jewish Power*.

[46] See Broder, 'Netanyahu and American Jews', p. 90.

[47] See Council on Foreign Relations, *US Middle East Policy and the Peace Process*, p. 20.

[48] The April 1998 letter to Clinton was sponsored by Senators Joseph Lieberman (Democrat, Connecticut) and Connie Mack (Republican, Florida). On the House letter of May 1998, see Knowlton, 'Mrs Clinton Starts Storm'.

Chapter 3

[1] See Hanns W. Maull, 'Alliance Cooperation and Conflict in the Middle East: The Gulf Experience', in Hanns W. Maull and Otto Pick (eds), *The Gulf War: Regional and International Dimensions* (London: Pinter, 1989), p. 147.

[2] For a useful study of various European policies in the Gulf War, see Gnesotto and Roper (eds), *Western Europe and the Gulf*.

[3] On continued US economic interaction with Iran despite the import ban, see Geoffrey Kemp, *Forever Enemies? American Policy and the Islamic Republic of Iran* (Washington DC: Carnegie Endowment for International Peace, 1994), p. 6. As late as 1994, US companies were buying $4.3bn of Iranian oil for resale in Europe. See Charles Lane, 'Germany's New Ostpolitik', *Foreign Affairs*, vol. 74, no. 6, November–December 1995, p. 77.

[4] Martin Indyk, 'Keynote Address: The Clinton Administration's Approach to the Middle East', speech delivered at the Washington

Institute for Near East Policy, Washington DC, 18 May 1993. Indyk became US Ambassador to Israel in 1995 and Assistant Secretary of State for Near East Affairs in 1997.

[5] On Iran's opposition to the peace process and how it affected US policy, see Fawas Gerges, 'Washington's Misguided Iran Policy', *Survival*, vol. 38, no. 4, Winter 1996–97, p. 7.

Chapter 4

[1] For the initial public articulation of the 'rogue-state' policy, see then US National Security Adviser Anthony Lake, 'Confronting Backlash States', *Foreign Affairs*, vol. 73, no. 2, March–April 1994, pp. 44–45.

[2] Reinhard Schlageintweit, 'Positive Approaches to Iran and Iraq', in *Report of the Trilateral Commission on the Middle East* (New York: Trilateral Commission, 1998), p. 12. Also see Franklin L. Lavin, 'Asphyxiation or Oxygen? The Sanctions Dilemma', *Foreign Policy*, no. 104, Autumn 1996, pp. 139–53.

[3] For a good example of this argument, see Gerges, 'Washington's Misguided Iran Policy', pp. 5–15.

[4] As stated in the 1996 Iran and Libya Sanctions Act (ILSA): 'It is the policy of the United States to deny Iran the ability to support acts of international terrorism and to fund the development and acquisition of weapons of mass destruction and the means to deliver them by limiting the development of Iran's ability to explore for, extract, refine, or transport by pipeline petroleum resources of Iran'. 'US Public Law 104–172: The Iran and Libya

Sanctions Act of 1996', Sec. 3 (a). Also see Lake, 'Confronting Backlash States'; former Director of Central Intelligence R. James Woolsey, 'Appeasement Will Only Encourage Iran', *Survival*, vol. 38, no. 4, Winter 1996–97, pp. 19–21; and Patrick Clawson, 'The Continuing Logic of Dual Containment', *ibid.*, vol. 40, no. 1, Spring 1998, pp. 33–47.

[5] *Reuters*, 2 October 1997.

[6] See Tom Buerkle, 'EU Recalls Envoys as Iran Is Found Guilty of Terror', *International Herald Tribune*, 11 April 1997, p. 1.

[7] Remarks by Secretary of State Madeleine Albright at Georgetown University, Washington DC, published as 'Preserving Principle and Safeguarding Stability: United States Policy Toward Iraq', US Department of State, 26 March 1997.

[8] For Italian Prime Minister Prodi's comment, see Brian Knowlton, 'US Sure of Allies If Saddam Reneges', *International Herald Tribune*, 26 February 1998, p. 1.

[9] For details, see *The Military Balance 1997/98* (Oxford: Oxford University Press for the IISS, 1997), pp. 26, 132, 139, 140; and Khalilzad, 'Challenges in the Greater Middle East', p. 195.

[10] See Lawrence G. Potter, *The Persian Gulf in Transition*, Headline Series No. 315 (New York: Foreign Policy Association, 1997), p. 66; updated for 1998 with unpublished IISS figures.

[11] Apparently confirming this French suspicion, the operation's name was changed from *Provide Comfort* to *Northern Watch*.

[12] Gulf analyst Michael Eisenstadt calls military deterrence of Iran an 'often unstated element' of US policy, acknowledging, as US officials are reluctant to do, that

while most US forces in the Gulf are there to contain and deter Iraq, they are also deployed to deter Iran. See Eisenstadt, *Iranian Military Power: Capabilities and Intentions* (Washington DC: Washington Institute for Near East Policy, 1996), p. 87.

[13] The British deployment eventually included the aircraft carrier *HMS Invincible*, 15 Naval strike aircraft and 8 Royal Air Force (RAF) *Tornado* fighter aircraft, 2,500 RAF and Navy personnel and other Naval, Army and RAF assets.

[14] Many French officials complained that the UK failed adequately to consult its European partners despite holding the rotating presidency of the EU at the time. According to the *Financial Times*, the UK was 'not known to have sought any mandate from the council of ministers before, or indeed after, sending forces to join those of the US in threatening air strikes against Iraq'. See 'EU and Iraq', *Financial Times*, 10 February 1998, p. 21. George Robertson quoted in *ibid.*

[15] See 'Europeans are Reluctant to Back Hard Line', *The Guardian*, 12 February 1998, p. 13; and 'Allies Promising to Support a US Strike', *International Herald Tribune*, 14–15 February 1998, p. 5.

[16] Prodi quoted in Maurizio Molinari, 'Prodi: Faremo il Nostro Dovere di Alleati', *La Stampa*, 18 February 1998; Italian official quoted in John Vinocur, 'Europe's Stance on Iraq: A Patchwork of Attitudes', *International Herald Tribune*, 13 February 1998, p. 1.

[17] See 'France Adds Pressure On Saddam to Yield', *ibid.*, 30 January 1998, p. 6.

[18] On 5 February 1998, Foreign Minister Védrine announced that France had 'no intention of associating itself with a military action against Iraq', and no intention of providing logistical support. See Mouna Naïm, 'La France ne Croit pas en l'Efficacité de la Manière Forte', *Le Monde*, 6 February 1998; and 'Hubert versus Madeleine', *Le Figaro*, 6 February 1998.

[19] The first poll was conducted by BVA for *Paris-Match*, and is available at www.yahoo.fr/promotions/sondages/irak2.html; the second was published in *Le Figaro*, 23 February 1998, p. 5.

[20] For the poll result and the quote from *Libération*, see Anne Swardson, 'US Ally Plays Role in Averting Airstrikes', *Washington Post*, 25 February 1998, p. A22. For the quote from *Le Monde*, see Mouna Naïm, 'La France se Réjouit d'Avoir Contribué à Faire Prévaloir la "Logique Diplomatique"', *Le Monde*, 25 February 1998, p. 3.

[21] See the interview with Chirac in 'M Chirac Plaide pour la Fin des Sanctions si l'Irak "Joue le Jeu"', *ibid.*, 27 February 1998, p. 2.

[22] See Gary Sick, 'Rethinking Dual Containment', *Survival*, vol. 40, no. 1, Spring 1998, p. 9.

[23] ILSA, signed on 5 August 1996, provided for six possible types of sanctions, from which the President was obliged to impose at least two: 1) a ban on financial support from the Export–Import Bank; 2) a ban on export licences for technology; 3) a ban on loans from US financial institutions; 4) prohibitions on financial institutions; 5) a ban on US government procurement from sanctioned persons; and 6) additional sanctions to restrict imports. In August 1997, the threshold for sanctions fell from $40m to $20m.

[24] See Leon Brittan quoted in Tom Buerkle, 'EU Steps Up Campaign Against US Sanctions; In Rebuff to Clinton, Bloc Taking Dispute to World Trade Body', *International Herald Tribune*, 2 October 1996, p. 1. For other examples of European criticism of the US' Iran policy, see Malcolm Rifkind, 'Secondary Boycotts are Not a Good Way to Fight Terrorism', *Washington Post*, 30 May 1996; and 'L'Europe Refuse que Washington Sanctionne des Firmes Etrangères', *Le Monde*, 7 August 1996, p. 2.

[25] UN Security Council Resolution 687, paragraph 22, states that 'upon the approval by the Council of the programme called for in paragraph 19 [the creation of a Fund to pay compensation to Kuwait] and upon Council agreement that Iraq has completed all actions contemplated in paragraphs 8 to 13 [the disarmament provisions], the prohibitions against the import of commodities and products originating in Iraq … shall have no further force or effect'.

[26] Védrine added that these conditions had already been met for nuclear weapons and '98% met' for ballistic missiles, though on chemical and biological weapons Iraq still had a long way to go. See the interview with Védrine, 'Entretien du Ministre des Affaires Etrangères, M Hubert Védrine', *La Tribune*, 27 April 1998. Other French statements refer not only to compliance with Resolution 687 bringing about a lifting of the oil embargo, but also stating that it was a 'necessary and sufficient condition for Iraq's reintegration into the international community'. See French Embassy in the United Kingdom, 'France and the Crisis of the Presidential Sites in Iraq', available at www.ambafrance.org.uk.

[27] Chirac refers to his letter in 'M Chirac Plaide pour la Fin des Sanctions'.

[28] As one senior British diplomat has put it, 'The US links sanctions with Saddam; the UK says compliance is the issue. In practice there is no difference, since Saddam will never comply.' Interview with British official, September 1997. In November 1996, then UK Foreign Secretary Rifkind suggested that the isolation of Iraq could end when a new government was installed that fairly represented the Iraqi people and respected human rights. However, he stopped short of explicitly linking Iraq's isolation to Saddam's departure. See Michael Binyon, 'Rifkind "Flies Kite" for Middle East Security Grouping', *The Times*, 5 November 1996, p. 13.

[29] See Johannes Reissner, 'Europe, the United States and the Persian Gulf', in Blackwill and Stürmer (eds), *Allies Divided*, p. 129.

[30] See Mouna Naïm, 'La Légitimité d'un Recours à la Force sans Nouveau Texte de l'ONU est Discutable', *Le Monde*, 22–23 February 1998, p. 3.

[31] See Laurent Zecchini, 'Washington Interprète la Résolution de l'ONU sur l'Irak comme un Droit de Riposte Automatique', *ibid.*, 5 March 1998, p. 3; and Jacques Amalric and Pierre Haski, 'Irak: La France S'Oppose à une Frappe Automatique', *Libération*, 27 February 1998.

[32] See Joseph Fitchett, 'US Is Said to be Reviewing Its "Containment" Policy on Iran', *International Herald Tribune*, 21 March 1997, p. 2.

[33] Compare, for example, the seminal study by Gary Clyde

Hufbauer, Jeffrey J. Schott and Kimberly Ann Elliot, *Economic Sanctions Reconsidered: History and Current Policy* (Washington DC: Institute for International Economics, 1990), and the critique in Robert Pape, 'Why Economic Sanctions Do Not Work', *International Security*, vol. 22, no. 2, Autumn 1997, pp. 90–136. Also see Richard N. Haass (ed.), *Economic Sanctions and American Diplomacy* (Washington DC: Brookings Institution Press for the Council on Foreign Relations, 1998).

[34] For a good discussion of the domestic politics behind ILSA, see Laurie Laude, 'Second Thoughts', *International Economy*, May–June 1997, pp. 44–70.

[35] Only 25% of those polled were opposed. See the *Wall Street Journal*/National Broadcasting Company (NBC) poll cited in Peter Rudolf, *Konflikt Oder Koordination? Die USA, Iran und die Deutsch–Amerikanischen Beziehungen* (Ebenhausen: Stiftung Wissenschaft und Politik, 1996), p. 18. A 1998 poll showed that 75% of Americans supported sanctions on Iran and Libya whether or not US allies agreed, compared to 21% who only supported sanctions that were backed by allies. See the poll cited in Patrick Clawson, 'What Next for ILSA?', *Financial Times Middle East Energy*, no. 19, January 1998, p. 16.

[36] See Sick, 'Rethinking Dual Containment', p. 9.

[37] International Monetary Fund (IMF), *Direction of Trade Statistics Quarterly* (Washington DC: IMF, June 1998), p. 127.

[38] Data on trade with Iran and Libya can be found in IMF, *Direction of Trade Statistics Yearbook, 1997* (Washington DC: IMF, 1997).

[39] On Iran's external debt, and continued European financing for Iranian projects, see Alan Friedman, 'Europe and Japan Are Guaranteeing $5 Billion in Loans, Tehran Reports', *International Herald Tribune*, 3 February 1997, p. 1.

[40] Figures on the Iraqi debt and trade with France provided by the Direction des Relations Economiques Extérieures, French Ministry of Finance.

[41] See Potter, *The Persian Gulf in Transition*, p. 62.

[42] See Lake, 'Confronting Backlash States', p. 46.

[43] See David C. Gompert and Richard Kugler, 'Free-Rider Redux', *Foreign Affairs*, vol. 74, no. 1, January–February 1995, pp. 7–12.

[44] Secretary of State Albright quoted in Richard Lambert, 'Big Partner Takes Care Not to Rock the Boat', *Financial Times*, 5 January 1998.

[45] For an interesting discussion of the crusading American tendency to try to shape the world for the better, see Walter McDougall, 'Back to Bedrock: The Eight Traditions of American Statecraft', *Foreign Affairs*, vol. 76, no. 2, March–April 1997, pp. 134–46.

[46] See John M. Goshko, 'Diplomats Perceive Iraqi Edge Against UN', *Washington Post*, 15 August 1998, p. A16; and Barton Gellman, 'Shift on Iraq May Signify Trade-Off', *ibid.*, 17 August 1998, p. A1.

[47] See John M. Goshko, 'US Rejects Move to Ease Iraq Policy', *ibid.*, 28 April 1998, p. A13.

[48] See the remarks by National Security Council official Bruce Riedel, 'US Policy in the Gulf: Five Years of Dual Containment', *PolicyWatch*, no. 315, Washington Institute for Near East Policy, 8 May 1998.

[49] For two of President Khatami's

most notable interventions on these issues, see his December 1997 speech to the Organisation of the Islamic Conference, in *BBC Summary of World Broadcasts, The Middle East* (SWB/ME), D3101/S1, 15 December 1997; and his unprecedented interview on Cable News Network (CNN), 7 January 1998, published as 'Transcript of Interview with Iranian President Mohammad Khatami', *CNN Web*, 7 January 1998, available at www.cnn.com.
[50] See Riedel, 'US Policy in the Gulf'.
[51] See Robert Corzine and Robin Allen, 'US Seeks to Mend Fences with Tehran', *Financial Times*, 19 June 1998. For earlier signals, see Elaine Sciolino, 'Quietly, America Takes Steps to Answer an Iranian Opening', *International Herald Tribune*, 27 March 1998, p. 12.
[52] Private copy of text of speech given by Representative Lee Hamilton, the ranking Democratic Member on the House Committee on International Relations, Council on Foreign Relations, Washington DC, 15 April 1998. Hamilton stressed the damage being done to US firms by the unilateral US sanctions on Iran.
[53] See Robert H. Pelletreau, 'European–American Cooperation in the Middle East', *Report of the Trilateral Commission on the Middle East*, p. 9.
[54] See 'European Declaration on Iran', *EU Press Release No. 26–27*, 29 April 1997; and Michael Lelyveld, 'Clinton Considers Waiving Iran Sanctions for EU', *Journal of Commerce*, 7 October 1997, pp. 1A, 5A.
[55] See 'Statement by the Secretary of State, Iran and Libya Sanctions Act (ILSA): Decision in the South Pars Case', US Department of State, London, 18 May 1998.
[56] See David White, 'EU Groups Welcome Deal on US Sanctions', *Financial Times*, 19 May 1998, p. 7; and 'Transatlantic Relations', *ibid.*, p. 27. In her statement, Albright made it clear that: she was not granting the general country-wide waiver in ILSA section 4c; that the US still opposed the South Pars investment; and that the US reserved the right to impose sanctions against other investments, particularly in pipelines that would cross Iran.
[57] See Thomas W. Lippman, 'Senators Press Clinton to Seek Sanctions over Iran Oil Deal', *International Herald Tribune*, 11 May 1998, p. 6.
[58] The vote on the bill was 392–22 in the House of Representatives and 90–4 in the Senate. See Nancy Dunne, 'Clinton Vetoes Sanctions Law', *Financial Times*, 25 June 1998.
[59] Similar proposals can be found in Shahram Chubin, 'US Policy Towards Iran Should Change – But it Probably Won't', *Survival*, vol. 38, no. 4, Winter 1996–97, pp. 16–18; and Rudolf, *Konflikt Oder Koordination*, pp. 26–29.

Conclusion

[1] See Anne Swardson, 'US Ally Plays Role in Averting Airstrikes: The French Hail UN–Iraqi Agreement as a Triumph – For France', *Washington Post*, 25 February 1998, p. A22.
[2] At a 28 May 1998 press briefing, Presidential spokesman Mike McCurry stated that the unilateral declaration of a Palestinian state would be an 'unfortunate development ... contrary to the agreements that the Palestinian Authority and the Israelis have

reached', and added that the US 'would most likely not join it'. This followed a statement ten days earlier by Assistant Secretary of State Indyk that the US would 'insist' that issues such as Palestinian statehood be resolved by the parties and not unilaterally. In a 23 June letter to the Conference of Presidents of Major American Jewish Organizations, Clinton reportedly wrote that the issue of a Palestinian state 'can *only* be settled through negotiations between Israel and the Palestinians'. See 'Press Briefing by Mike McCurry', The White House, Office of the Press Secretary, 28 May 1998; Robert Satloff, 'New Nuances', *The New Republic*, vol. 219, no. 2, 13 July 1998, p. 15; and Matthew Dorf, 'Would Clinton Recognize a Palestinian State?', *Washington Jewish Week*, 23 July 1998, p. 8.

[3] For details, see US Mission to the European Union, 'The New Transatlantic Agenda' and 'Joint US–EU Action Plan', Press Releases, Public Affairs Office, 3 December 1995.

About **The Transatlantic Allies and the Changing Middle East**

Since the mid-1990s, US and European attitudes, strategies and policies towards the Middle East have diverged. In the Middle East peace process, Europeans have grown frustrated with the lack of progress and Washington's near-monopoly on diplomatic action, and have begun to demand a greater role. On Iraq, the US insists on Saddam Hussein's military and economic containment, while some Europeans have started to press for a more rapid reintegration of Iraq into the international community and are reluctant to use or threaten force. The issue of how to deal with Iran has been most divisive, with the US threatening to impose economic sanctions on its European allies to coerce them into following Washington's harder line. This paper examines the reasons for these potentially damaging differences, assesses the prospects for improving transatlantic cooperation in the region, and suggests approaches that may help to bring this about.

About **The International Institute for Strategic Studies**

The International Institute for Strategic Studies is an independent centre for research, information and debate on the problems of conflict, however caused, that have, or potentially have, an important military content. The Council and Staff of the Institute are international and its membership is drawn from over 90 countries. The Institute is independent and it alone decides what activities to conduct. It owes no allegiance to any government, any group of governments or any political or other organisation. The IISS stresses rigorous research with a forward-looking policy orientation and places particular emphasis on bringing new perspectives to the strategic debate.

For Product Safety Concerns and Information please contact
our EU representative GPSR@taylorandfrancis.com Taylor & Francis
Verlag GmbH, Kaufingerstraße 24, 80331 München, Germany

T - #0161 - 270225 - C0 - 234/156/5 - PB - 9780199223770 - Gloss Lamination